RSA

THE MONEY BAZAAR

THE MONEY BAZAAR

Inside the Trillion-Dollar World of Currency Trading

ANDREW J. KRIEGER

WITH EDWARD CLAFLIN

T I M E S BOOKS

Grateful acknowledgment is made to the Institute for Interna-
tional Economics for permission to reprint one chart from *Dollar
Politics: Exchange Rate Policymaking in the United States* by
I. M. Destler and C. Randall Henning (Washington: Institute for
International Economics, 1989, p. 25). Reprinted by permission.

Library of Congress Cataloging-in-Publication Data

Krieger, Andrew J.
The money bazaar : inside the trillion-dollar world of currency
trading / Andrew J. Krieger with Edward Claflin.—1st ed.
p.   cm.
Includes index.
ISBN 0-8129-1861-4
1. Foreign exchange futures.   I. Claflin, Edward.   II. Title.
HG3853.K75   1992
332.4'5—dc20   91-50593

Manufactured in the United States of America

9   8   7   6   5   4   3   2

FIRST EDITION

To my parents

for their unwavering love

and encouragement

Acknowledgments

I WAS COMPELLED to write this book for two reasons.

The first, from my conviction that the foreign-exchange market is the most significant market in the world—affecting in subtle but distinct ways every aspect of economic and social order in the United States and the other nations of the world. I wanted to create a book that would describe what brought this market into being, to reflect on what forces move it, and to sketch out the evolutionary path in which it may be heading.

The second and more important reason was that once I started the process, there were a number of people who would have been enormously disappointed if I didn't finish; people who generously provided their time and skills to help bring it into being. What began as a

Acknowledgments

vague concept was transformed into a reality by their sheer persistence—and it is difficult to imagine how this metamorphosis could have occurred otherwise. I would like to thank them all, and I apologize to any whom I have inadvertently overlooked.

I am most grateful to Jane Dystel, my agent, who initiated the project, and to Shlomo Maital, Ph.D. (of the Technion, MIT, and Brookings Institute), who provided valued assistance and commentary at every stage of development.

I owe special thanks to Edward Claflin, who explored the esoterica of currency trading with unfailing determination and helped shape the book from mountains of interviews and research. I cannot imagine a better collaboration.

There were many who provided important information and commentary to both of us, and a number of people who reviewed various drafts in great detail. I was fortunate to have extensive support and valued critiques from my partner, Jon Berg, and I am grateful to all those in my office who combined energies daily to triumph over the dark forces of chaos—Peter Molyneux, Eileen Pabon, Barbara Keller, Sheri Gorin Baker, A. J. Kleeger, Dawn Latawiec, Kim Coates, and Michele Zevits. My thanks, also, to Everett Ehrlich, James Barnes, Richard Munoz, and Walter Chang for their valued assistance

Acknowledgments

to Edward Claflin in helping to shape the background material.

My enjoyment of currency trading is, perhaps, somewhat easier to understand if one realizes that this market has more than its share of remarkably articulate individuals keenly attuned to world events and economic change. They are only a phone call away—and the calls were numerous. Friends, contacts, investors, competitors, traders, brokers, skeptics, and believers, I appreciate your patience, forbearance, humor, and wisdom.

I would like to offer words of special appreciation to Wilhelm Halbfass for his many years of struggle in trying to guide me toward acquiring the discipline to think and write in a cohesive fashion, and to Indira Devi for trying to provide me with the inner fortitude to persist when darkness is blocking my path.

My wife and children have been unfailing pillars of support of this and all of my other projects, and a heartfelt word of thanks is offered to them. I know that this project has taken much time that would otherwise have been spent with them. This has been the main sacrifice of the endeavor.

My first adventure in the world of publishing took a number of unexpected turns, and I was fortunate to have Peter Osnos, publisher of Times Books, steadily pressing this book through the hairpins. Fortunate, too, is the

Acknowledgments

writer who gets to work with Steve Wasserman, editorial director of Times Books. He and his editorial assistant, Peter Smith, gave the manuscript the careful shaping and pruning it needed—and their efforts proved essential in the all-important final stages of this two-year commitment.

Contents

	Introduction	3
1	The Money Bazaar	14
2	Habits of the Market	27
3	Understanding Capital Flows	46
4	Anticipating Trends	52
5	The Dialectics of Decision Making	82
6	Bretton Woods and All That	105
7	Genghis Khan's Dilemma	117
8	All That Glitters Is Not Gold	135
9	Brave New World	149
10	The Floating Dollar	160
11	The Force	172
12	The Boiled-Frog Syndrome	182

Contents

13 One Nation, Under Debt   190

14 Living with Uncertainty   200

    Conclusion   210

    INDEX   225

THE MONEY BAZAAR

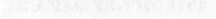

Introduction

I HAVE A NIGHTMARE.

It begins one evening when I am at home in my study, watching prices on the Reuters screen. A foreign-exchange trader from Tokyo is on the phone.

Suddenly the line goes dead.

I try to phone him back. No luck. I try another number—this time, a bank in the heart of Tokyo. Again, no response. I keep dialing. Each unsuccessful call deepens my dread. Tokyo is down. No one is getting through.

Then my phone rings. "Andy, have you heard? There's been an earthquake in Tokyo. No one knows how bad it is yet."

Throughout the night and into the early morning hours, a new scenario is played out on the foreign-exchange market—the kind of scenario that has never before occurred in the history of the market.

Within hours, traders have begun a massive sell-off of the yen. These traders know that many Japanese investments, worth tens of trillions of yen, are supported by property in the overinflated Tokyo real estate market, which is held as collateral. They realize that if Tokyo is in ruins, the Japanese stock exchange, the Nikkei, will virtually collapse. Even the largest of Japanese banks is likely to fail. Japanese investment houses—overleveraged in both real estate and securities—will crumble as their capital base vanishes.

And what will happen when traders around the world begin selling yen? As they establish their positions, the market will be flooded with the Japanese currency, creating a gross oversupply. Prices will tumble. Investors will vie frantically to unload their yen assets before the currency spirals lower and lower in waves of panicked selling.

As I imagine the nightmare happening, leaders of Japanese government and industry meet in the ruins of a devastated capital. Privately, they agree to shore up their collapsing currency in the only way possible, with a massive buy-back of yen in the foreign-exchange centers around the world.

Slowly and quietly at first, then with accelerating

speed, the Japanese begin to purchase yen, liquidating huge amounts of their foreign-currency holdings.

In this nightmare, more than $500 billion worth of yen is repatriated within a few days. By the time the buying spree is over, trillions of yen have been ripped out of the market and bonds and money-market instruments around the world have been devastated, crumbling under the unprecedented selling pressure.

There's no liquidity. Traders, investors, commercial banks, and central banks are caught short of billions of dollars' worth of yen, with no sellers to be found. The yen, which was in free-fall, now has an unprecedented, explosive rally against every major currency. Traders are wiped out overnight; liquidity dries up and all markets come to a virtual standstill.

In 1982, when I entered Wharton Business School, I had no intention of becoming a foreign-exchange trader. I had graduated from the University of Pennsylvania in 1978 with a major in philosophy. After graduation, I did a stint on the professional European tennis circuit, then returned to Penn at age twenty-three to begin working for my master's in South Asian Languages and Cultural Studies. As a graduate student, I pursued studies in Eastern philosophical thought. I also studied Sanskrit, Bengali, Arabic, and Hebrew.

For a time, I worked toward my doctorate completing my coursework and the translation of an obscure Sanskrit text; with the plan of becoming a professor. Some soul searching, followed by discussions with a number of professionals in the field, made me conclude that I wasn't cut out for academic life. Although my grades were excellent, I did not look forward to a life filled with hours of lonely research. In 1982, newly married, I entered the M.B.A. program at the Wharton Business School. I had no specific ideas about what I would do afterward, but I needed to make a living.

While at Wharton, I took a summer job trading money-market instruments with a subsidiary of J. P. Morgan & Co. in Wilmington, Delaware. I enjoyed the intricacies of the market, especially options trading. Before the next semester began, I was offered an opportunity to work with the investment firm of O'Connor and Associates in Chicago. I took a leave of absence from Wharton and moved to Chicago to learn options trading at the Chicago Board Options Exchange. Still working for O'Connor, but back in Philadelphia, I began trading currency options on the Philadelphia Stock Exchange.

In 1984 I completed my MBA and took a job with Salomon Brothers in New York. After the training course, I began trading in the foreign-exchange area. I moved to Bankers Trust in 1986, where I remained through the end of 1987. I left in February 1988, after a year in which Bankers' foreign-currency profits amounted to $512.8 million, up from $57.4 million the previous year. (In 1988, Bankers' foreign-currency profits were $153.9 million.)

In March a front-page article appeared in *The Wall Street Journal* under the headline "Change of Heart: Andrew Krieger Made $3 Million Last Year—Why Isn't He Happy?" In the article—and in other stories that appeared in the press—there was much speculation about why I had left Bankers Trust. Was I disgruntled with the bonus I had received at Bankers? Had I riled the bank's directors with excessive trading activities? Were there secret losses that would be revealed only after I left?

The truth was banal and far less exciting. I needed a break. During three years of intense and steady trading, I had been glued to the computer screens, telephone in hand, eighteen to twenty-two hours a day, six days a week. I had traded every major currency and tested numerous strategies—some successfully, others less so. The profits were real—but so was my exhaustion. Was this really what I wanted to do for the rest of my life?

For a time, I believed I would give up trading. I had bought a farm in the Catskills as a much-needed retreat for my family and me. I began reading and studying again. But by the end of 1988, I had set up my own investment firm in Englewood Cliffs, New Jersey. I began consulting for a number of private and institutional investors.

Today, I am still a participant in the market. There are weeks when I trade nearly around the clock. Almost nightly, my telephone rings at two or three in the morning. At home, at my farm, and of course in my office, I have Reuters screens that constantly monitor the prices of the world's leading currencies. I confess: I'm hooked. In this book, I want to tell why.

What is the lure of this market? What is its power? How did foreign exchange grow to be the most important market in the world? What are its inherent dangers?

To many people, currency trading seems at best a kind of alchemy and at worst like Vegas-style gambling. It is a market with its own language, run by "insiders." It proceeds at a hectic pace. The amounts traded seem spectacularly large: foreign-currency traders may move ten million, a hundred million, or a billion dollars at a time. Yet for all its mysteries, it is simply a market like any other. In this market there are elements of both science and gambling, but foreign-exchange trading is neither.

There is little doubt that this market affects every aspect of our daily lives and influences the economic and political destiny of every nation. In that sense, I believe it is essential to have some understanding of how it

Introduction

works. Here's why: The U. S. dollar in your pocket is, almost literally, your stock in America. Like stock, its value fluctuates on the international market, depending on the level at which it is being traded at any particular time. It has a bid price and an asking price. Day and night, some traders are buying dollars ("going long the dollar") while others are selling ("going short"), and the dollar's value fluctuates constantly as a result of this free-market activity.

How do those fluctuations affect the buying power of your dollar? What happens when there is a great deal of demand for this American "stock"—and therefore its price increases? Or what happens when supply outruns demand, when there are more sellers than buyers, and the value of the dollar declines? How, exactly, does that affect your personal purchasing power? And what impact does the rise and fall of this "stock in America" have on the health of the nation as a whole?

As the dollar changes value by infinitesimal amounts throughout the day and night, the accumulated shift in buying power could amount to 10 or 20 percent (or more) during the course of a year. But what is the real impact of those changes on prices, salaries, and savings? How does a currency devaluation or revaluation actually affect the way we lead our lives?

If we experience inflation during the year, we can see it happening. Prices go up at the grocery store, at the mall, at the car dealer's. But how do we detect the fact that the dollar has risen or fallen against the pound, the yen, or the deutsche mark? And why should we care?

Well, for one thing, we might care who owns pieces of America—more specifically, who owns U.S. Treasury bonds, equities, private property, manufacturing plants, and other assets that are accessible to foreign investors. Over time, exchange rates play a large role in determining who helps pay for our government deficits, who buys equity in U.S. companies, who owns the building on your corner, who hires the person next door, and who owns the bank that handles your accounts.

If it turns out that some entity from a foreign country is paying your salary, buying your products or services, or investing in your local economy, you can be certain that foreign-exchange rates have a great deal to do with the decision to make these kinds of investments. When our currency becomes devalued, our human, natural, and commercial resources look increasingly attractive to overseas buyers.

Foreign-exchange rates also affect prices. Numerous items on the racks and shelves of your local stores are shipped from elsewhere. What you pay for a television from Japan, a coat made in Hong Kong, or a car made in Germany is directly influenced by the relative exchange rates of those currencies. During 1986, when the yen rose 24 percent against the dollar, the base price of a Toyota Camry leaped 13.4 percent, from $9,378 to $10,648. A Seiko man's watch that cost $115 in January 1986 rose 17.4 percent, costing $135 twelve months later. Even though Japanese companies went to extraordinary lengths to cut production costs, hold down prices, and subsidize their exports, the American consumer still bore the brunt of the exchange-rate hit.

Since the deutsche mark and the French franc also rose as the dollar collapsed, we also paid more for German and French imports. That BMW 528E you wanted to buy for $26,280 in January 1986 cost 7.8 percent more in January 1987. Your five pounds of French Roquefort cheese rose 13.4 percent in the same period, from $7.49 to $8.49. With lower-than-ever savings (we spendthrift Americans saved less than 4 percent of our take-home pay), we dug out our credit cards and borrowed to pay the price increases brought on by dollar devaluation.

Foreign-exchange rates also affect exports, of course, and our export trade is crucial to domestic prosperity. When the dollar reaches stratospheric heights against other currencies, as it did during 1984 and early 1985, the prices of American goods we sell all around the world are effectively raised, as foreigners are able to purchase fewer items with the same quantity of foreign currency. The export market begins to dry up. Given a choice between equivalent items, people will buy cheaper products rather than pay a premium for American-made goods. And we're caught, because if we lower prices too much, we can't make a profit in our export business. We eventually slow production for foreign markets. When production falls, layoffs begin. Perhaps worst of all (in terms of farsightedness), we slow our efforts to design and market products destined for foreign markets. Whenever we reduce exports because of foreign-exchange inefficiencies, our net income diminishes and the *future* of our export business is also hurt.

Theoretically, one could imagine a group of sage advisers sitting down at a table to measure market forces, then deciding on exchange rates and interest rates that would make sense for all the nations involved in international trade. In brute actuality, however, exchange rates are determined by free-market forces, with governments running interference whenever things begin to get too nasty. Diplomacy plays a role in such decision making, but the day-to-day decisions that affect the value of the currency in your pocket are resolved by personalities and institutions that have no hand to guide them.

The market has its own momentum; it follows its own imperatives, and it arrives at its own conclusions. Since those conclusions, fortunately or unfortunately, affect the value of the dollar in your pocket, it's advantageous to have some understanding of how these forces are related.

In this book I try to address these issues—and also raise questions about the behavior and efficiency of this free-market foreign-exchange system.

My nightmare of a global market collapse may never become a reality. I certainly hope that it doesn't. Yet, whether such an occurrence is likely or unlikely, it lies in all our interests to be aware of what this market is, what it does—and how it guides today's world with its invincible hand.

1

The Money Bazaar

ACCORDING TO 1991 estimates, the foreign-exchange market is a trillion-dollar-a-week money bazaar. Its daily transactions range between $500 billion and $700 billion. It is, without question, the largest free market in the world.

Economically, the globe is divided, for better or for worse, into "hard" and "soft" currencies. The dollar, for instance, is hard. The Brazilian cruzeiro—to take the other extreme—is soft. With dollars in your pocket, you have a currency that will be useful in Brazil and anywhere else in the world. Dollars have value far beyond the borders of the United States. Cruzeiros, on the other hand, are useful in Brazil, but that's about it.

In theory, cruzeiros have exchange-rate value. You can read about their theoretical value in the exchange-rate columns of *The Times* of London or *The Wall Street Journal*. But that is only a theoretical exchange rate. In order to actually exchange cruzeiros for hard currencies, you have to find a buyer, and that may be extremely difficult. A London merchant banker does not want cruzeiros, and neither does a Wall Street securities broker. If a Brazilian citizen can find a way to change cruzeiros to dollars and come to his London banker or New York broker with dollars in hand, the financiers who deal in hard currency will talk. But the Brazilian currency itself is "good" only inside Brazil—and even there it is less valued than American dollars, British pounds, German marks, Japanese yen, and other hard currencies.

On the foreign-exchange market, where volume trading takes place, dollars, marks, yen, Swiss and French francs, and other hard currencies are bought and sold by traders using telephones, telexes, and Reuters machines. In this market, most of the capital is provided by banks, multinational corporations, and investment firms—though anyone with sufficient capital can enter the market. (There are a number of very sizable and active private investors.) Size-wise, the foreign-exchange market dwarfs the combined operations of the New York, London, Frankfurt, and Tokyo stock exchanges.

Although regarded as a single entity, the foreign-exchange market has no central headquarters or clearinghouse for trades. When the market "opens" in Sydney, Australia, for example, it means only that traders are at their terminals in Sydney's banks, ready to make bids and offers on all major currencies. Though morning in Sydney is near the end of the business day in New York, a Wall Street trader can begin trading by phone in the Australian market and continue his trading activities as the markets open in Tokyo, Hong Kong, Bahrain, Geneva, Frankfurt, Paris, London, New York, and finally Los Angeles and San Francisco; and he can still be at his desk when the market opens in Sydney again.

As a whole, then, there is only one foreign-exchange market. Traders observe the indicated "bid" and "offered" prices—as well as updated financial and international news—on a computer screen that is linked to the Reuters or Telerate network, but the real market transactions take place on a direct interbank basis or through currency brokers. Most traders keep track of stock and bond prices as well as some commodity prices, since trading in all markets has a direct or indirect bearing on currency prices. Essentially, there is one massive pool of international capital that flows from one investment vehicle to another, and it is this shifting of capital that ultimately drives the currency rates. It is for this reason that currency traders pay such close attention to the performance of other markets. But the foreign-exchange market is a separate entity.

Anyone with a telephone and a line of credit can

play. Most trading is done verbally, and any voice agreement to buy or sell is binding. Though a limited amount of trading is now being done by computer—with electronic verification of trades—the one-on-one voice contact is still the primary form of transaction.

In a typical transaction, a trader from Citibank in New York might call Midland Bank in London and ask for a price on a certain quantity of dollars versus deutsche marks—say, $10 million in deutsche marks. The London dealer provides a dealing price—the price at which he is willing to sell dollars (the offer) and the price at which he is willing to buy dollars (the bid).

If the Citibank trader buys $10 million at an offered price of, say, 1.4945, then he sells DM 14,945,000. The dollars are credited to Citibank's account, and the deutsche marks are credited to Midland's account.

Now the New York trader has a number of opportunities. If the dollar should rally—that is, if it rises immediately—he might resell the U.S. currency to the same London bank or to a different buyer anywhere in the world. In other words, the trader at Citibank might decide to liquidate his position by selling out his dollars and buying deutsche marks, thereby earning his profit.

Suppose the dollar rallies up to 1.50 deutsche marks (DM 1.50). When the Citibank trader sells out his $10 million, he then gets back DM 15 million. That leaves him a net profit of DM 55,000. When he liquidates DM

55,000 at the market rate of 1.50, it gives him a profit of $36,666.67.

The aggregate of thousands of such transactions taking place every minute of the day finally has an effect on the dollar in your pocket. If you were using that dollar only to buy domestic products sold in the United States, then it would effectively be immune to exchange-rate fluctuations. If Idaho potatoes, for instance, become more expensive to produce and ship, those costs are likely to be passed along to you, the consumer, in the form of higher prices. On the other hand, if those domestic costs decrease, or Idaho has a bumper crop this year, you are likely to be able to buy potatoes at a lower price. In other words, the Idaho-potato-buying power of your dollar is largely a function of domestic variables within the potato industry and the U.S. economy.

But few products sold in the United States these days are as homegrown as Idaho potatoes. At your local appliance store, the U.S. dollar buys TVs, VCRs, microwave ovens, radios, tape recorders, and CD players produced and assembled in Korea, Taiwan, Japan, Hong Kong, Mexico, Canada, and other corners of the globe. In each of those countries, capital expenditures on plant and equipment are paid in the local currency. Workers, too, are paid not in dollars, but in the currency of their own nations.

The U.S. importer who brings such goods to America

pays, of course, in dollars—which are then changed into the foreign currency so that the producer can be paid. When the foreign-exchange rate favors imports (i.e., when there is a strong domestic currency), lower import costs will soon be passed along to you, the consumer, in the form of cheaper TVs and lower-priced microwave ovens. Looked at another way, the dollar's buying power serves as a global clearing mechanism wherein the powerful forces of international trade and monetary exchange, combined with the profit motive, conspire, on a worldwide basis, to bring the most attractively priced goods in the world to your appliance store.

In the reality of the American market, few goods or products are immune from the influence of foreign-exchange rates. Nearly every major industry—from manufacturers of mainframe computers to assemblers of children's toys—utilizes imported products or components. Conversely, a large percentage of domestic production is devoted to export sales. And that production includes more than commodities: it also encompasses numerous kinds of services, from educating foreign students to fighting oil-well fires.

Forty years ago, the United States was a kind of factory-warehouse, supplying a vast array of goods and services that were shipped to neighbors near and far. Today, the nation is an enthusiastic participant in a flourishing import-export business. We still produce, of course, and some of our products still are exclusively homegrown. But above all, we buy, sell, and consume.

In this new world of global trade, then, virtually all products and services are directly influenced by international monetary exchange rates. Foreign investment and trade are inextricably linked to daily life in America. When we buy cars, we choose among models that are manufactured in Sweden, Great Britain, Germany, France, Italy, South Korea, and, of course, Japan. Most cars made by the Big Three in the United States include many parts that are made and/or assembled in other countries. Our selection of food, clothing, building supplies, raw materials, and assembly-line machinery reflects the diversity of our imports. Reading labels from goods on our national shelf, one can almost fill in a map of the world.

But the dimensions of the U.S. import-export business extend far beyond store-bought goods. To an extent unimaginable four decades ago, foreign investment in the United States has changed the shape of our domestic economy. Large blocks of commercial and private real estate are wholly or partially owned by the British, Dutch, Canadians, Germans, Japanese, and others. The manufacturing and service sectors depend heavily on investment from overseas. U.S. commodities, bonds, and securities are directly affected by foreign investment. Every aspect of industrial, commercial, and economic activity in the United States reflects, to some degree, the interaction between America and foreign nations.

Therefore, the weight of the U.S. dollar against foreign currencies plays a vital role in all aspects of trading activity. The 1980s was a decade when the dollar's value measured against other leading currencies rose to astounding heights, then plummeted, dropping over 50 percent in the span of a few years. This was also a decade in which the foreign-exchange market saw explosive growth. The United States emerged from the decade unable to assume or maintain a role as global leader in establishing monetary policy.

Radical shifts in the dollar's value, uncontrolled by a "dollar policy," are possible because the foreign-exchange market is a free market in the purest sense. If the dollar in your pocket loses half its international buying power during the next five years, that tangible shift in equity will not be the result of any planned, procedural intervention decided upon by a cabal of international conspirators. Rather, it will be the sum of the activities of more than two hundred thousand active traders in the foreign-exchange market, plus millions of global investors and participants in multinational trade.

There are no restrictions in this market. No single international authority acts as a governing body, and no government can intervene unilaterally to regulate for-eign-exchange practices or—should there be a threat of a world monetary crisis—to halt trading.

The foreign-exchange market, then, is the one stabi-lizing factor in the world's system of monetary exchange, yet it is not answerable to any extrinsic stabilizing influ-ence. While treasury officials in Washington, London, Bonn, Tokyo, and other capitals pay close attention to relative currency values, none can directly intervene in a regulatory capacity. While traders, brokers, and other participants voluntarily follow certain conventions, hab-its, and rituals in their trading and investment activities, none is answerable to any authority higher than the institutions that employ them. Since there are no "seats" in the international foreign-exchange market, it is impos-sible to "unseat" a trader—much less expel a trading institution—for violation of accepted practices.

This market was created not by design, but because traders, bankers, investors, importers, and exporters rec-ognized a chance to make money. In 1971 the United States went off the gold standard. At that moment, new profit-making opportunities appeared on the horizon. When exchange rates ceased to be under international control, a global trading system sprang up to answer a need. Absent restraining forces, that market became self-perpetuating—increasing in size in direct proportion to the increase in opportunities for investment, growth, and profit.

That burgeoning market provides liquidity. An American importer buying Japanese goods must trade dollars for yen in order to pay for those goods. The German buying American goods must sell deutsche marks and buy dollars in order to pay his invoice with U.S. currency. Thanks to the foreign-exchange market, dollars, marks, yen, and all other leading currencies are available in vast supply. The liquidity of this market has answered handsomely to the global demands for currency during an era of unprecedented growth in world trade.

The fascination of this market lies in its size, its complexity, and the almost limitless reach of its influence. During the past decade, the foreign-exchange market has been the invincible hand guiding the purchase and sale of goods, services, and raw materials in every corner of the globe. The behavior of that market can send a signal to foreign investors to buy U.S. property, corporations, and financial instruments; conversely, its behavior can motivate U.S. corporations to expand their exports or invest capital overseas. During some periods, currency fluctuations may induce foreign nationals to purchase American assets; at other times, it can force them to adopt stricter austerity measures at home—to produce at lower cost, to lower their profits, or to seek new avenues of export.

As you read this page, the activities of the foreign-exchange market are changing the value of the dollar in microadjustments that may eventually have a very large impact on the world you live in. During the coming decade, the activities of this market will help determine whether your dollar continues to give you access to a global supply of products sold in America. It will restrain or unleash the sale of American assets to buyers around the world. In large part, the foreign-exchange market will help decide how rapidly and successfully Eastern Europe is rebuilt. It will react to the economic unification of Western Europe; to the interplay of economic and social forces in Japan and Southeast Asia; to the ongoing conflicts in the Middle East.

The foreign-exchange market is both reactive and predictive. Its behavior will measure economic and political events ranging from small changes in interest rates to large social and political upheavals. The market's response to global events will then have a direct impact on the fates of nations by helping to determine the health of their economies and their relative power vis-à-vis their neighbors.

Like other free markets, the foreign-exchange market shares the potential for shifts, corrections, and strong trends. When there is net demand, the price must rise.

When there is oversupply, the price falls. The fact that this market deals in currencies certainly introduces a complication into the usual market equation, and it increases the variables. But the nature of the commodity being traded—dollars, pounds, deutsche marks, and other currencies—does not alter the fundamental supply–demand functions that underpin any free market.

Whatever the outcome of the next decade, as long as there is an unregulated foreign-exchange market, the value of the dollar in your pocket will unquestionably rise and fall—hence, the rationale for calling it your stock in America. At the most basic level, when its value rises against other leading currencies, you will have greater international buying power. Imported goods and services will be cheaper, and if the dollar's rise continues, an increasing number and variety of those goods are likely to be imported. On the other hand, when the dollar declines in value, foreign goods are likely to become more expensive, as will domestically produced goods with foreign-produced components. Should the dollar remain devalued for a significant length of time, fewer goods will be available; you will have a narrower range of choices. To put it bluntly, your life-style will suffer, and so, quite likely, will your standard of living.

Along with the impact visible to the consumer, however, the implications of dollar revaluation and devaluation extend beyond mere purchasing power. Among the variables is the question of international position and prestige. How *much* of America do we want to sell? For how many years can we continue having a net trade deficit with other leading industrial nations? What should be the premium value on a U.S. dollar when it is used by other nations as a currency of convenience? How much good can be gained from devaluation in terms of expanded foreign trade?

These questions go beyond import-export considerations. They are linked to our status as a nation and our place in the world. That status is constantly being tested, analyzed, and revised by the foreign-exchange market. The price of the dollar in terms of other currencies is both a reflection and a function of America's future.

2

Habits of the Market

I MAY HAVE LEARNED more about the foreign-exchange markets studying Eastern religion than I did at Wharton Business School. At Wharton, everything we needed to know about the foreign-exchange market was dealt with in a cursory, rudimentary fashion in International Finance. It was hardly mentioned in the course on speculative markets, since Spec Markets focused primarily on whether one could speculate in the equity markets and make money over time. In fact, we studied efficient market hypotheses and were taught that we could not consistently make money in freely traded markets through speculation. No professor said anything about making money in foreign exchange.

After going through the training program at Salomon Brothers, I started out in the foreign-exchange area. At that point, I had developed some skills in the area of computer programming and systems design, with a specialization in options theory, and I put the background to work in structuring my trading strategies. I had nothing to go on except my knowledge of options theory and an intuitive feel for the markets.

I was fortunate in having an excellent manager, Gil, who was a particularly skillful trader in bonds and fixed income instruments. Foreign exchange was a new game for him, but he had terrific instincts about markets and people. For a young trader such as myself, he was the perfect manager. He gave me plenty of room to grow and express myself in creative ways, and he made sure I had the finest analytical support systems available. He also taught me about the interrelationships of markets and encouraged me to look at the bond and commodity markets as a way of understanding and forecasting currency flows. I started following the trading in crude oil, soybeans, and other commodities even while I was exclusively trading currencies.

For instance, at one point Gil noted that speculators had started buying soybeans, which he said was an indication that people were worried about inflation. But instead of investing in soybeans, Gil began buying the Swiss franc. When I asked him about it, he told me, "Whenever there's inflation, people move toward traditional safe havens like the Swiss franc. It makes sense that the Swiss franc is going to go up." Sure enough, it did, and Gil took profits on his position in Swiss francs.

I began to get the sense that there was a huge pool of money out there looking for ways to invest or speculate to earn the highest yield. Noting how the markets were interrelated gave me a profound respect for the hidden power they exert over all our lives. I kept expecting someone to step in and tell me the rules. That never happened. By implication, therefore, I discovered that the main function of my job was to discover the rules by myself.

Part of my early training was spent learning the conventions that apply to currency trading. For instance, British pounds are called "cable," a throwback to the days when trading with London was done via transatlantic cable. The price on cable is expressed in terms of dollars. In 1984, the price was close to 1.1550—in other words, one dollar, fifteen and a half cents to the pound.

I learned that Japanese yen, German marks, Swiss francs, and most other currencies (with the exception of Australian and New Zealand dollars) are expressed in terms *relative to* the U.S. dollar. Instead of saying that the deutsche mark is trading at .6666 dollars per deutsche mark, traders worldwide will say that the deutsche mark is "at 1.50"—meaning that one dollar is worth 1.50 deutsche marks per dollar.

At the end of 1984, the pound was trading around

1.1590 (dollars per pound sterling); the yen was trading around 251.50 (yen per dollar); the deutsche mark was at 3.1460 (marks per dollar); and the Swiss franc was at 2.6010 (Swiss francs per dollar). If I called for prices on any of these currencies, I would be given only the last two digits ("ninety," "fifty," "sixty," or "ten"). The dealer or broker would assume I knew the rest of the price, i.e., the "handle." For example, if I asked for a price in "dollar-Swiss," I might hear "Ten–twenty," shorthand for 2.6010–2.6020, the dealer's bid–ask spread between where he wants to buy and sell dollars *versus* Swiss francs.

Like traders in other markets, foreign-exchange traders think in terms of "going long" in one currency and "going short" in another—that is, in relative terms. If people are buying currency A and selling currency B, then they are "going long" currency A and "going short" currency B. A is in demand (bid) while B is in supply (offered). The relative values of A and B are therefore always changing. If currency A is strengthening against currency B, it is being revalued relative to currency B; if B is weakening, it is being devalued relative to currency A.

Since British pounds sterling are expressed in dollars, the dollar is strengthening when the pound's price hits a *lower* number. That is, if the price moves from 1.160

to 1.150, the pound is weaker, the dollar stronger. In most other currencies, the dollar is strengthening when the price moves to a *higher* number. If dollar/deutsche mark goes from DM 1.45 to DM 1.55, the dollar is strengthening and the mark is weakening. Or, to take it the other way, if the dollar/yen is "at 140" (that is, trading at 140 yen per dollar) when it was previously "at 280," then the yen has doubled in value, as measured against the dollar.

Looking at the price of cable on the Reuters screen in 1984, I might see the numbers 1.1540/50—that is, the pound is offered at $1.1550 if I'm buying and bid at $1.1540 if I'm selling. If the market is fairly stable and my Reuters terminal is working properly, I will expect the bid and ask prices given to me by the broker or dealer to be close to the same spread as the prices on the screen.

When I call my counterparty for a price, I do not necessarily let the dealer know whether I am a potential buyer or a seller. I simply say:

"Price on twenty pounds, please."

In shorthand, I have just asked for the price of 20 million pounds sterling. With those few words I imply that I am ready to deal in this amount, and if the dealer shows me a reasonable price, I will either buy or sell. But the dealer does not know my preference until I make a trade. He also takes for granted (since I haven't mentioned otherwise) that I am dealing "spot." Whatever deal I make, the actual exchange of dollars for pounds—the "delivery"—will occur in two banking days.

Suppose he says, "One-fifteen, forty–fifty."

His reply tells me that the dealer is prepared to sell me 20 million pounds sterling at $1.1550. And the dealer is ready to *buy* from me 20 million pounds at $1.1540 if I happen to be selling. The difference between these prices is the "spread."

If I say, "At forty!" I am the seller of 20 million British pounds. Each pound is sold at $1.1540.

"Agreed. At 1.1540, you sell 20 million pounds."

"Thank you."

I jot down my "fill"—the price at which the order is filled—on a trading sheet. And then we either talk about our families, sporting events, the state of the world, and imminent invasions of Third World countries, or else I hang up.

These 20 million pounds have generated $23,080,000. Now I am "short" pounds and "long" dollars. To "cover" I will have to sell dollars and buy pounds. And when I do that, I'll be "square."

My goal, of course, is to hold my sterling "position" until the pound decreases in value, then buy back my pounds at a profit when I cover.

It is difficult for any counterparty to know the extent

of my profits on a transaction. It might be that I bought those same 20 million pounds sterling at $1.1500. Now, by selling sterling at $1.1540, I am making a profit of $.0040 on each pound sterling, for a total profit of $80,000.

On the other hand, if I buy pounds at $1.1550, I might have sold them earlier at $1.1600, and now I am repurchasing them for a gain of $.0050. That will put me $100,000 in the black on that particular deal.

By January 1985 I was trading around the clock. In general, my major plays in the market were structured using long option strategies. When one purchases a currency option, one then has a right—but not an obligation—to buy or sell a currency at a fixed price at some date in the future (usually no longer than one year). By using option strategies, I could structure my trades such that the maximum amount of money I could lose on any one market play would be the amount of premium I spent on the option. This was an advantage because the profits were potentially unlimited—to the extent that the market moved my way.

In currency trading, using options is a way for investors to reduce their risk. Options can also be used by traders to take a risk position for the sole purpose of realizing profits. While the actual trading of options can be quite complex and involve sophisticated mathematical models of risk and return, the principles are fairly straightforward:

Options—whether in currencies, commodities, or securities—give someone a right but not an obligation to buy or sell a fixed amount of something at a fixed price on or before a future date. If I try to sell you a bag of oranges for $1.20 when the market price is $1.10, you won't take the offer. Why pay ten cents more than the market price?

But what if I sell you the right to buy oranges for $1.20 a bag three months from now? In other words, for a premium—the price of the option—you can buy oranges at $1.20 in ninety days. And let's say I set the price of that premium at an attractively low figure. What if I said that for a premium of three cents (the option price), you could buy oranges at $1.20 in ninety days.

Now your decision whether to buy the option on oranges reflects your opinion about future conditions in the market. If you think there's a good chance—a high probability—that oranges will go up to $1.30 in ninety days, then you'll accept my offer. For three cents per bag, you get the option to buy at $1.20 and then sell them at $1.30. So you make seven cents on each bag of oranges. Or you can consume oranges at a cost of $1.23 ($1.20 price + $.03 option) at a time when your neighbors are paying $1.30.

(As a practical matter, one bag of oranges is much too small to deal with commercially; so, instead, we strike a deal for one "lot" of oranges—say, a hundred thousand bags. And every time I sell you "one orange" I'm actually selling one contract-size lot of one hundred thousand bags of oranges. Or, in trader's shorthand, I say, "I'll offer one ninety-day orange call at 3.")

That, in fact, is the essence of commodity options— the kind that have been traded on the Chicago commodities exchanges for more than a hundred years. When I started trading, similar options were being offered in currencies. For a certain defined premium, I could buy a "call" option—a contingent asset, a right (but not an obligation) to purchase yen, deutsche marks, Swiss francs, or other currencies against the dollar at a specific date in the future. I could also buy a "put"—a contingent liability, an option that gave me the right to sell a currency. If I own a lot of oranges that I've already paid for, I'm "long" oranges. (And I'm "short" the cash that it took to buy them.) On the other hand, if the dollars are still in my pocket and I haven't bought any oranges yet, I'm long dollars and short oranges.

For currency traders, options trading opened up new realms of possibilities. Now they had as many derivative instruments to utilize as traders in the other financial markets. To the options trader, volatility is an important factor. If the price of oranges looks as though it's going to remain stable—that is, there will be a low level of volatility in the market—traders have little incentive to buy an option of any kind. In times of volatility, or in times when traders foresee volatility, option purchases become increasingly costly as they reflect the increased probability of the market players needing some price protection.

The premium I pay on the orange option—that is, three cents per bag—is really the insurance premium I pay in order to have the opportunity to buy oranges at $1.20 per lot, just in case the price of oranges skyrockets in the next three months. I need oranges for my business, and the three-cent premium may well be worth the outlay as a protective mechanism.

If I pay three cents for a call, I'm saying, "Yes, I think prices may go significantly higher." In fact, I want the price to go lower since I need to buy the oranges no matter what, and I would rather buy them at a cheaper price. My overall break-even point on this transaction is $1.23, or the strike price—$1.20—plus the three-cent premium.

If I pay that price for a "put," I'm still saying I expect price movement—but my hedging requirement is against a lower price instead of a higher one.

And if I buy both a put and a call, I'm taking a more neutral view, saying, "I don't know which way prices are going to move but I think there will be a large change; so I'm planning to cover myself in both directions."

There are infinite trading possibilities in options. What if the option is mispriced—that is, on a theoretical basis, the three cents is either more or less than it should be? Perhaps one option is priced at a level that's too high or low relative to another option because of a short-term supply-demand imbalance. This often occurs when a large speculator purchases or sells a large quantity of a particular option contact. The option trader may then spread, or sell (buy) this overpriced (underpriced) option while buying (selling) a different, fairly priced option.

Many probabilities are involved. One must assess not only the direction in which the spot market will move, but also the manner in which it will behave. Will there be sharp, dramatic changes in direction over a relatively narrow range, or will there be a steady price appreciation or depreciation?

Once I have worked out the market's probable price behavior, then I can examine the option premiums and decide whether I think the option values are too high or too low. Obviously, I won't want to buy an option that is overpriced. In the original work that I did on options while studying at Wharton, my primary concern was to build a model for determining which options were relatively overpriced—with a view to seeking a system that would identify strategies based on the spreading of mispriced options. Later on, after I had acquired some practical trading experience, I developed a personal abhorrence to selling options, which complicated my job as a trader. I dislike the idea of holding unlimited downside risk in exchange for a limited upside premium payment. Therefore, in actual trading practice, I tend to use spreading strategies when volatilities are high, while I often use simple option purchases when they are at cheap levels; but I am always net long of options. My downside risk is always defined and limited.

On a very large play, I might spend several million dollars on one strategy. Generally, I would be making a directional bet—that is, calculating that the dollar would move in one direction or another versus the yen, the pound, or the deutsche mark. If those currencies were to go in the opposite direction, I would risk the amount that I had spent on the option. But if they were to go my way, I could take very large profits.

Needless to say, I could not spend $1 million or $2 million flippantly on an option play. One runs out of money very soon if one loses several million dollars regularly.

During the last half of the eighties, I would make the bulk of my money from five or six major plays every year. The rest of the time I would generally be testing the waters and probing for market opportunities.

The markets offered tremendous profit-making opportunities during the mid-1980s. Huge adjustments in the dollar's value and equally massive shifts in cross-currency (non-dollar) relationships were commonplace. Once I understood what was going on, I began to note how people did extraordinarily stupid things in the market—myself included, of course. In general, whenever something was going up, the traders got bullish, and whenever it was going down, they got bearish. By sitting and observing and talking to friends in the market, I could see that people's views were often shortsighted. I began to piece together scenarios that indicated when sharp reversals might occur. In other words, if it looked as if there would be a rally after a sell-off, I would countertrade to catch the rally. Vast quantities of money were moving around, and many of these opportunities arose because of frenzied speculative activities and the ensuing volatility.

From the beginning of my trading career, I particularly enjoyed making contact with traders around the world. By early 1985 I had trading relations with banks in New York, Singapore, London, Sydney, Zurich, and Tokyo. My network of information and contacts extended to many other places as well. I had good relationships in Frankfurt, and I did business in Toronto, Los Angeles, Chicago, Hong Kong, even Bahrain. I could find out what was going on and execute business in any time zone.

Developing a dealing relationship with another bank is like making a cold call. First a trader checks to make sure the other bank has an established credit line. Then he calls and introduces himself. This is as simple as saying, "Hi, this is Andy from Salomon Brothers in New York. I was wondering if I could talk to someone about setting up a dealing relationship and doing some business."

One of the counterparty's salespeople would get on the phone line. As the salesperson and I got to know each other, we would start doing business. Eventually he and I would begin calling each other with ideas or information.

In practice, I would trade spot-currency business with other banks in exchange for their information about the order flows and market news. In making these calls, I found that almost anything I chose to discuss with foreign traders would eventually have some bearing on my trading. Having open lines to all corners of the world gave me an opportunity to gain knowledge about other cultures. I learned about the educational system in Singapore. About family life in Japan. About gambling practices in Hong Kong. About the Swiss banking system. I got British opinions on the French, the Germans, the Americans, and the Japanese. And I heard many opinions about political, economic, and military situations in every hemisphere. Some of this information applied directly to foreign-exchange trading; some didn't. But ultimately, it all seemed relevant. The world had a pulse, and I had my thumb on it.

By mid-February 1985, I had a portfolio that reflected both long-term and short-term views. Beginning January 1981, when Ronald Reagan had become president, the dollar made a steady overall appreciation against other leading currencies. The eleven months from March 1984 to February 1985 were particularly dramatic, with an appreciation of nearly 20 percent against other leading currencies.

I felt the dollar had reached its peak and was about to begin a dramatic descent; but I knew it was difficult and dangerous to sell into a powerful bull market. I was completely focused on the structure of my portfolio, and I was always trying to figure out the best way to increase my profits to the fullest extent possible. Though I had no way of knowing it then, the market was about to make some unprecedented moves.

In late 1984 and early 1985, the dollar had exceeded the highs that anyone believed possible—and still it kept on climbing, as it headed for one of the steepest cliffs of all time.

Though most traders thought the dollar was overvalued, no one knew when the sell-off would begin. In February 1985 the dollar peaked, then declined sharply. It lost about 6 percent during the next month, recovered slightly, then started down again. By September 1985 it was off nearly 13 percent from its February high.

On Sunday, September 22, 1985, financial ministers from five countries met at the Plaza Hotel in New York to discuss exchange rates. The "Group of Five" (G-5) consisted of representatives from the United States, Japan, Germany, France, and Great Britain. On the evening of September 22, this group announced the terms of the "Plaza Agreement," which stated that "further orderly appreciation of the main non-dollar currencies against the dollar is desirable."

Immediately, the dollar went into an unprecedented twenty-four-hour plunge of 4.29 percent against the world's leading currencies. At the end of trading on Monday, the dollar closed at 2.689 German marks, a 5.3 percent change from the 2.8395 close the previous Friday. At the same time, the yen soared from 238.50 to 225.68.

During the next two years, the dollar continued to depreciate against other major currencies, including the British pound, the deutsche mark, the yen, the Swiss franc, and the French franc. By early 1987 it was exactly where it had started six years before, when the Reagan administration had first announced that it would not intervene in exchange-rate matters. From February 1985 to February 1987 the dollar fell some 50 percent, measured against the world's leading currencies. In international terms, the net buying power of every individual in the United States was reduced by half.

By the time the G-5 made its grand appearance, I had begun to develop a broader historical perspective on the markets. Through painstaking research I had accumulated price data on currencies going back to the First World War, and I had begun to examine certain patterns and cycles.

What I saw was not comforting.

The charts, the hitchhiker's guide to the galaxy of trading, are graphs that show the trading history of various currencies, as maintained by assorted data bases, central banks, and financial institutions around the world.

On the vertical ("Y") axis of each graph is the exchange-rate expressed in *Currency A per Currency B*— that is, yen per dollar, deutsche mark per dollar, and so on. The horizontal ("X") axis lists days, months, or years. If one wants a microview of how a particular currency has been trading recently, one selects a chart that spans anywhere from one day to six months. For a longer view of how currencies have been behaving over many years, a trader uses a chart that spans a decade or more.

True "chartists" are those who religiously study their graphs on a daily basis and generally look at past behavior as a reliable predictor of the market's future performance. Based on their interpretation of the charts' structure, chartists will trade accordingly. In my case, my rather cursory study of the historical charts showed that, given certain possible world developments, almost any type of currency movement was possible.

In fact, after the Plaza Agreement and continuing through the better part of 1987, a rarely used word began to appear with increasing frequency in the financial press.

That word was "free-fall."

Traders, like most people, are creatures of habit. After the dollar has moved in one direction for a number of months, market players note that in order to make money it is easiest to simply go with the trend; that is, to assume the trend will continue. Traders become habituated to trading with either long or short dollar positions, and they will continue this habit until a series of losses convinces them that the trend has reversed. When a reversal finally comes, everyone rushes to get out.

Each major upturn or downturn is the result of some pressure building up on the market. In actuality, there are no prescribed limits to the movement in foreign exchange. The leaders of the industrialized countries might *wish* the dollar were at a certain level relative to the yen or the deutsche mark, but in fact they have no way to enforce their wishes.

To a trader experiencing the aftereffects of the Plaza Agreement, it was apparent that the foreign-exchange market could behave like a supertanker out of control. There was plenty of activity on board—but no one at the helm.

3

Understanding Capital Flows

IN ANALYZING THE MARKET, it is always hard to determine the forces that cause investors to shift their asset allocations. With an international pool of investment opportunities and a large group of individuals and institutions prepared to make investments, various market signals can alter the flows of capital. And whenever there is a major shift in capital flows, it has an effect on currencies.

In other words, simply shifting assets from one country to another will affect a currency's value. If Swiss investors decide to decrease their asset holdings in U.S. investments and increase their asset holdings in Japanese investments, then the dollar *versus* the yen is likely to depreciate. The net shifting of capital flows coupled with the net shifting in trade flows drives the market. So it is important to understand what criteria are being used by individuals to make their investment decisions—in other words, what decisions *cause* the capital flows.

Many of the capital flows are speculative in nature, but the real investment adjustments are massive. In other words, there are many investors who are trading simply to make profits in foreign-exchange transactions. But there are others who need the foreign exchange for liquidity—that is, they are trading currencies simply because they need to do so in order to carry out business in various parts of the world.

A speculative investor is a trader who has the job of capitalizing on the short-term flows. For instance, the dollar/deutsche mark dealer who sits at the foreign-exchange desk of a major bank like Citibank focuses exclusively on the relationship of the dollar to the deutsche mark. His job is to figure out what his customers are likely to do during the course of the day, anticipate price movements, and position himself properly. If the dollar/deutsche mark dealer is expecting a net demand for the dollar against the deutsche mark, then he will be long the dollar until he thinks the dollar has moved up as far as it's likely to go. At that point, he will liquidate his position and take some profits.

Although his activities are purely speculative, he is creating liquidity for investors and for corporate accounts that need to manage their requirements. In the process, he tries to anticipate how prices are likely to shift as a wide range of investors and corporate users go about their business every day.

In contrast to speculative trading, many of the transactions on the foreign-exchange market are commercial ones that are required for a company in one country to do business with another. Suppose, for instance, that ImportCo in the United States wants to purchase Jaguars from Britain. ImportCo has to buy British pounds in order to pay for the Jaguars. The question is, how should ImportCo manage its currency risk? Should the company buy pounds today to pay for the cars, or should it buy the pounds in three months when it takes delivery of the cars?

Some companies, taking a passive approach, simply "hedge up" as soon as the currency requirement is known. For example, if the dollar/sterling rate stands at 1.70 today and ImportCo knows it will have to pay £20,000 for each Jaguar it purchases in Britain, then the dollar cost per Jaguar is $34,000. Of course, rather than settling its account on the day the contract is written, ImportCo would rather wait three months and pay on delivery. But ImportCo doesn't know what will happen to the pound during the next three months.

On the one hand, the pound might appreciate considerably—let's say as much as 7 or 8 percent. In that case, the purchase price (in dollar terms) would be far higher. So if ImportCo waits to buy pounds, it runs a risk of seriously cutting into its own profits. Conversely, if the pound should depreciate during that period, ImportCo would be able to buy pounds much more cheaply, lowering its cost per car and thereby increasing its earnings.

But there is a way ImportCo can guard against this risk, even in an ever-fluctuating currency market, and still postpone payment until it takes delivery of the Jaguars. That method is universally known as hedging. To hedge its investment, ImportCo "buys sterling forward" for the day it has to make payment on the cars. ImportCo gets from a currency dealer an outright "forward rate," which is the price quoted for delivery of the currency in three months. For instance, if the rate is 1.70, then ImportCo knows that its cost in ninety days will be $34,000 per car. No matter which direction the pound goes—up or down against the dollar—ImportCo has stripped out the currency risk. The only remaining question is what price the importer can get for Jaguars in the United States once it has taken delivery.

So the treasurer at ImportCo calls up one of the banks at which he has a prearranged currency line allowing him to buy or sell forward currency. He asks what the price will be on a certain amount of British pounds for delivery three months hence. Given a price of 1.70 (dollars per pound) on a forward basis, the treasurer simply says, "At 170, I would like to buy three million pounds for September 16 settlement." The dealer at the bank gives a verbal confirmation. Then a fax is sent from the bank to the customer, specifying how many dollars have to be sent to the bank on September 16 in order to make payment for the pounds. And the deal is done.

In other words, it is a necessary and efficient commercial transaction that enables the importer to hedge his currency risk by taking out a forward contract. The bank makes no commission. It simply buys pounds at one price and sells at another, making a profit on the "spread" in each transaction. For instance, if another customer comes in and sells pounds to the bank at 1.6990, which the bank then sells to ImportCo at 1.7000 it earns 10 points on the £3 million, for a total of $3,000. The active bank dealer who handles commercial accounts is like the retailer who wants to keep inventory moving: He is buying and selling as much as he can, and trying to make a little profit on each transaction.

However, ImportCo has not stripped out *all* future currency risks: Next year, when ImportCo's treasurer buys the pound, the price may have fluctuated adversely. If the pound rallies, his British Jaguars might cost $40,000 or $45,000. This is a major consideration in ImportCo's future projections—a consideration that may, in fact, dominate all other business risks.

If the pound were to rally by 20 percent, the currency component of ImportCo's business could render it non-competitive. The nature of the global interdependence of American business is such that the profitability of companies like ImportCo may depend on how sophisticated the treasurer is in making decisions about long-term currency movements.

4

Anticipating Trends

A FOREIGN-EXCHANGE TRADER, whether speculating, investing, or hedging on behalf of a corporate client, is constantly trying to anticipate trends in the market. To do this he must look at a wide range of factors, including relative interest rates, inflation, and political and economic factors in leading-currency nations. Government, treasury, and central bank policies also affect price action in the market. In addition, it is important for a trader to be aware of the psychology of markets in general—to understand, to whatever degree possible, why certain trends develop and which facts, rumors, and events are likely to influence other participants.

To focus on just one of these factors, a U.S. trader must consider what portion of capital flows in and out of the United States is in the form of investment dollars seeking favorable real interest rates. The real rate is the nominal rate minus the effects of inflation. If someone invests in a U.S. interest-bearing vehicle when the nominal interest rate is 10 percent and inflation is 5 percent, the real interest rate is just 5 percent. International investors in general are looking for currencies in countries where economic growth is strong, inflation is low, and real interest rates are high. The perfect combination of all three rarely exists—and then only for brief periods of time. However, to the degree that a nation's economy offers these attractions, more people are likely to purchase that nation's currency in order to take advantage of investment opportunities.

Once a trend gets started, it becomes a habit. The saying "Big ships turn slowly" is especially applicable to the foreign-exchange market—the biggest ship in the world. Once it starts moving in a powerful way, it is unlikely to reverse quickly. People do not give up their habits easily.

When the market starts to develop a trend, traders get used to certain kinds of habitual price and trading behaviors. For example, when the dollar is in a bear market against the yen and it starts going down, people feel fairly safe that the market movement is likely to continue that way. Traders sell the dollar first with the hope of buying it back later for a profit. Even if they sell at slightly lower levels and the dollar rallies against them a bit, they feel sure that the dollar will come back down again. When a lot of traders are selling, they combine to create tremendous downward pressure on a currency.

At a certain point, however, the ship has gone as far as it can, and it has to refuel. In other words, the market has to assess whether the trend is going to continue. One factor that might influence that assessment is whether fundamental economic conditions have changed. Has the United States moved out of a recession and started a growth phase? Have relative interest rates started to shift? If so—if traders anticipate a shift in relative interest rates or relative economic performance—that anticipation may itself have a large effect on currencies.

To take an example from recent history, in early 1991 the dollar rose sharply against other leading currencies. Though the domestic U.S. economy was in bad shape, investors became convinced that growth in Europe was slowing and the U.S. recession was about to end. They also expected that relative interest rates and relative growth rates were going to shift in favor of the United States. Therefore, dollar-denominated assets became more attractive, because investors thought fundamental market conditions would improve in the United States and decline elsewhere. Capital began pouring into the United States, and traders were forced to purchase dollars as the demand for dollars created a surge of its value against other currencies in the market.

However, any trader who is dealing in a number of currencies must consider *which* currency seems most promising and *when* he should time his activities. To say "The dollar is strong" is an oversimplification. While it might be strong against some currencies, it could be weak against others.

Once a trader arrives at a market view, he still has to fine-tune his decisions. If I want to buy dollars against deutsche marks, for instance, at what price do I want to buy them? Just because I want to buy them at some time doesn't necessarily mean that moment is now.

There are levels at which I want to buy dollars and levels at which I want to sell them. I determine in my own mind the parameters for the market, based on prior market experience and certain types of price action that are probable in terms of the magnitude of movements. If I have a bias toward buying dollars, for instance, I want to buy them when they turn back to levels of support; and when I want to sell them, it should be when they are rising toward levels of resistance. Some of the levels of resistance might be the same "highs" the dollar reached ten or fifteen years ago. On the other hand, the dollar might have already touched some of those levels three or four weeks ago.

Before I make any trade, I have predetermined at what level I think my idea is wrong, and I will liquidate my position if the market reaches that level. I know that if I buy dollars against deutsche marks and the dollar then goes beneath a certain level, it is not behaving as I expected. Therefore I'll move over to the sidelines.

Or, if the dollar goes up to a certain level, then I'm likely to take profits. The market's inherent validity must be respected, as the market is always right.

When should I get in? When should I take profits? And when should I cut my losses? These questions are part of an ongoing dialectic. That dialectic is never as simple as "I think it's going up, so I intend to buy it." Instead, I'm likely to say to myself, "I think it's going to go up, so I'm going to buy at such and such a price—or I'm not going to buy it at all."

Currency charts are particularly helpful in showing historical levels of resistance. For instance, in 1985 the dollar reached a level of 3.48 against the deutsche mark—and after that, in a matter of a year, it plummeted over 200 pfennigs. What happened was that the dollar reached a high that was completely rejected by the market, and once that level was rejected, it never climbed up there again.

Similarly, the pound never went below 1.03 against the dollar. Once it touched that level, it climbed to £2.00 in a matter of years. So, for the pound, 1.03 is (to date) the all-time low.

In other words, certain highs and lows are important

levels in the market. Since markets are a function of supply and demand, there must be reasons that, collectively, all the players in the market reject certain levels. These are the "levels of resistance" that I consider when I am deciding how to trade.

In addition to considering economic factors, interest rates, and market history, a trader must also make allowances for the way markets behave in general. All markets go through accumulation and distribution phases. Accumulation occurs at certain levels where there is net demand. As the demand overwhelms the supply, the price goes up. When other traders see the price going up, they believe the market action is the start of a bigger trend and they say to themselves, "Let me buy some, too."

For example, suppose there's a market in apples with many people willing to buy or sell at certain levels. For apples priced at 10 cents, there are many eager buyers—but who is willing to sell at that price? At 20 cents, on the other hand, there are many people willing to sell, but who wants to buy at a price that high? To put it another way, there are net buyers "at 10" and net sellers "at 20."

But some of the people who were able to purchase apples at 10 are going to liquidate their positions— that is, sell their apples—when they are offered a higher price. So the net buyers at 10 are going to have partial liquidations as the price rallies toward 20 in order to realize some profit.

In an actual market situation, there might be a lot of buying and selling at 10, but the price doesn't go down. As the net demand continues to absorb the selling, the buyers—who aren't getting all they need—move their bid up to 11. The buying and selling continues, but the price doesn't go any lower. So the buyers move their bid up to 12.

Finally, the bid goes all the way up to 20. Now, shift to the point of view of speculators who have been watching this price action. They didn't understand the demand that moved the price from 10 to 20. But they might begin to start buying at 20 because they hope the market is going to go up to 30.

Meanwhile, some of the buyers who bought at 10, 11, or 12 step in and sell certain amounts at 18, 19, and 20. As the price moves down from 20, the speculators are forced to liquidate because the market is going against them. All this selling finally pushes the price down to 15.

Then, new buyers come in at the 15 level and there's good solid demand. These buyers were perhaps too timid when the price was at 10 and did not buy enough of their required apples at the lower levels. The current price of 15 is 25 percent cheaper than 20, so they are quite happy to begin buying now.

The new demand moves the price back up to 20, then 21, 22, 23, 24, and finally 25. At this point, the cycle begins to repeat itself: Speculators who have been observing the price action come in at 25, convinced the price will go to 30. But meanwhile, there's distribution from the people who bought on the way from 15 to 25—and as they start selling, the price starts coming back down again.

What makes this process somewhat comical is that the speculators who bought "at 20" the first time *were right*. But they were wrong about the timing of entry, because they misread the supply-demand function.

Nearly all markets display this "step" pattern—and the foreign-exchange market is no different. Of course, the "steps" can occur at any level. Since conditions are constantly changing and the variables are infinite, no chart can predict when supply will overreach demand and a retrenchment will occur.

Markets always seek equilibrium. In an unregulated market with adequate liquidity, eventually an equilibrium point will be found. For example, if the scale of the market is 10 to 20, at 10 there is tremendous demand, and at 20 there is tremendous supply. In other words, people who are willing to pay 20 will get all they need, because 20 is a good selling price. And if they are willing to sell at 10, they will find numerous buyers, because many people are willing to risk buying at 10 with the expectation that they can sell higher. On this scale 15 might be the neutral point—where people can probably buy or sell a large amount without having much of an impact.

In the currency market, as political and economic considerations shift, the neutral point can shift. Suppose, for example, the neutral point is 15 when there is a change in political leadership. The shift in the equilibrium point will depend on how buyers and sellers feel about the change in leadership. If people distrust the leader and believe he will lead the nation into monetary and political crises, the "neutral point" for trading that currency might shift from 15 to 11. On the other hand, if people like the new leader and trust his economic and political judgment, then the neutral point might become 19.

On this scale, if the United States were to move out of a recession into a booming recovery, if there were buoyancy in the economy, with real interest rates going up and inflation coming down, the neutral point might become 30. In other words, buyers could be found for the dollar, even though it would have a higher market value when measured against other currencies than has recently been the case. The equilibrium point keeps shifting because the world and the fundamentals of each economy are constantly in flux.

When I began trading currencies in 1984, the dollar was in the midst of a powerful upward trend. It seemed as if the dollar would just keep rising. But as it reached each new high, traders asked themselves, "Is this the peak? Or is it just going through some retrenchment before it continues up again?"

All of us were trying to understand where the 10, 15, and 20 were in this worldwide market. None of us wanted to be a new buyer at 20 when, at any moment, it might start down to 19, 18, or 17. On the other hand, all of us wanted to have part of the profits if it looked as if this market were headed toward 28, 29, or 30.

Which was the right entry point? And where should a trader get out?

An excellent example of this process can be gleaned from one of my experiences with the British pound.

Like the other European currencies that were affected by the rising dollar in the early 1980s, the British pound steadily lost ground. From July 1980 to September 1981, the pound depreciated 34 percent against the dollar. It had traded above $2.00 in 1980, but by 1985 it had plummeted to $1.04. In 1985 the pound started to recover, and it strengthened further after the Plaza Agreement. This movement had little to do with the British economy, however, as despite Margaret Thatcher's claims of prosperity, inflation and unemployment in the United Kingdom were still very high. Further, the British economy was afflicted with ongoing trade deficits.

The chancellor of the exchequer, Nigel Lawson, was concerned about the pound's weakness against the other European currencies as this exacerbated Britain's domestic inflationary pressures. While the strength of the pound against the dollar was aided by the dollar's sharp downward trend, raising the pound's value against the strong Swiss franc and powerful deutsche mark was much more difficult. The pound had weakened by about 25 percent against the deutsche mark between late 1985 and early 1987.

I had turned bullish on the dollar during the last week of 1987, when I was still at Bankers Trust. But I was also bullish on sterling against the mark and sterling against the Swiss franc. I thought that for technical reasons the pound was getting ready to soar.

The first week in January, there had been a massive dollar rally (which I was quite happy with, since I had been long dollars). Then in February 1988 there was a big rise in sterling against the mark and Swiss franc. By then, I had already left Bankers, but I was still watching the markets.

When I joined George Soros' Quantum Fund, I thought the dollar was trying to form a solid base. I knew that there were many large speculative short-dollar positions and that there was a good chance the dollar would rally strongly when these speculators began buying back their dollars.

Meanwhile, the pound had just finished an amazing rally of some 10 percent against the deutsche mark over a very short period of time. It had also rallied against the dollar. It looked to me like a boom-bust situation for the pound—and we were in the middle of the boom. All the speculators were getting themselves massively long in sterling. But why? The fundamentals of the British economy weren't strong enough to justify their optimism, and I thought the rally was going to be short-lived. I saw a sterling collapse coming, but when would it happen?

I talked to Soros about the situation. I told him I thought it was a boom-bust that was about to break apart. The fund already had one position in sterling. We were long about 500 million pounds of sterling call options with a $1.85 strike price, and the spot price was around the $1.88 level. I told Soros I thought we should sell pounds against those options. In addition, I thought we should start selling pounds outright against the dollar. His response was, "That sounds fine. You're the currency expert. When it starts going your way, really let 'em have it." Then he went off to Europe.

Shortly after I had joined the Quantum Fund, I asked Jeff Tuttle, an experienced currency dealer from Los Angeles, to come work with me. Since early April, we had been trading as a team. The Friday after I spoke with George, my trading partner told me he was pretty bearish on the dollar. "I'm particularly bullish on sterling," he added. "It looks to me like it's the strongest of all the currencies against the dollar. The dollar looks like hell."

"Jeff," I said, "I really hate sterling, but I'm sure you'll be disciplined in managing your positions, so go ahead and trade as you see fit."

I planned to trade the Standard & Poor's stock index futures that morning, so we went our separate ways. Even though we sat side by side at trading desks, we usually traded separately, conferring periodically about our respective positions. About 11:30 I decided to ask Jeff how he was doing.

"I'm fifty pounds, short," he said.

"Short?" After telling me he was bullish on the pound, he had spent the morning selling 50 million pounds.

"Well," he said, "I made a few calls. Everyone I talked to was bullish on the pound. I figured if we all were seeing the market in the same way, then we were probably all wrong, so I decided to sell some."

The pound had dropped a little, so his position was profitable, but I was amused that my trading partner was making money by trading against his own views. I was bearish on the pound myself, so we decided to sell some more pounds.

My partner had proceeded judiciously all morning,

easing out about £10 million every hour. It had taken him all morning to sell £50 million.

It only took us about twenty minutes to sell the next £250 million, as liquidity in the market was excellent.

Beginning the following Monday and, for the next two weeks, we continued to build up our positions slowly. Overall, my goal was to sell 500 million pounds against the options and an additional 400 million pounds in spot outright against the dollar. I was looking for a major blowout—almost a collapse of the pound.

My sales took place at good levels, generally between 1.8800 and 1.8950. I was a scale seller, gently putting on the positions. I would sell 10, 20, or 30 million pounds at a clip, trying not to disturb the market. I just wanted to get my initial 500 million pounds sold quietly.

In the market it was pretty well known that I had sold a lot of pounds. But the banks that were holding my positions for me couldn't believe that my positions were so large. They were unaccustomed to watching traders, leaving themselves open to multimillion-dollar profit-and-loss swings with every quarter of a percentage point price fluctuation. Every time the pound rallied up a penny or two, they would watch and wonder when I would get out. What these people did not realize was that my position was fully protected by a British pound call option that limited our losses.

Over a ten-day period I then sold the additional 400

million pounds for my spot position. Although there was no immediate reaction in the market to confirm my views, I continued to be negative on the pound. In fact, I was more and more certain it was going to plummet. The British trade figures were set to be released in the third week of May, and I thought the release of the data would be the catalyst to push the pound toward its inevitable fall.

This number was critical.

There was no doubt that Britain would show a trade deficit—the only question was how large the deficit would turn out to be. I figured it should be quite high—around £1.2 billion. If the number turned out to be higher than expected, the pound would break lower. On the other hand, if the trade deficit number was much lower than I expected, the pound would resume its unwarranted rally and I would be caught the wrong way around.

I went into the office early to be there when the trade figure was announced.

It was six in the morning, New York time—eleven in London.

During the morning in London, rumors had been circulating that there was going to be a good number. The market had begun pushing the pound up from the $1.87 level, and sterling was trading at $1.8770 when the trade figures were announced.

Then the trade figure was announced—transmitted to every currency-trader's screen and every terminal around the world. I couldn't believe the figure that came up on the screen. It was £525 million—less than *half* what I had expected. The deficit in British trade was *far* less than anyone expected.

It was a great number for England. But it was a horrible number for me. It meant that the fundamentals of the British economy—and therefore the fundamentals that were "holding up" the pound—had improved, and it meant that a lot of traders were going to turn still more bullish and try driving the pound higher and higher.

As I sat gazing at the screen, my stomach dropped. I felt as if all the energy was pouring from my body into the floor. I looked at my partner. There was a terrible pallor in his complexion. We both knew there was no way we quickly could buy back all those pounds without creating a panic. I saw my partner nudge the trash basket closer to his chair. "He's going to be sick," I thought.

I looked at the screen again, thinking, "Oh, God, that number is awful. It's going to be very, very unpleasant to buy all those pounds back." Thirty seconds later, the screen flickered again. The pound was still rallying. Up another full penny. It looked to me as if it would just keep going.

I was feeling nauseous, but I held on to my position. I said to myself, "I'll just wait and see what happens." I was also saying to myself, "There *must* be a better way to make a living." I couldn't have thought of a worse scenario for my positions; a wildly bullish market with a fabulous trade number. The currency continued to surge.

I realized that this would be a good test of how great the demand for sterling really was. It would also be a good test of my intestinal fortitude. If the pound failed on this rally, it would probably make a huge move down. All the short-term market conditions to drive it higher were now in place. If those conditions didn't drive it higher, it would show that my original theory was right in that the market was tremendously overbought and the pound was ready to collapse. As far as I could fathom, the long-term fundamentals didn't justify such a lofty currency level, but I was beginning to waver slightly in my convictions.

Suddenly the switchboard lit up like a Christmas tree. It was six thirty-five in the morning, and phone calls were pouring in. Sadistic traders from all over the world were calling me to drive their stakes into my heart.

I answered a line. The perky voice from London belonged to the chief dealer of a London branch of a U.S. bank in a major trading operation.

"Hey, mate, how're you doin'? What're you thinkin' here?"

"That was a great number, wasn't it?" I said.

"Yeah, yeah," he replied. "I think the pound's just going to roar."

"You know what," I said, "I think you're right. I think the pound's just going to go through the roof today. It's a much better number than expected. I think you have to be long pounds."

"Oh." He was clearly surprised by my candor. That trader knew I was short pounds, as news of my short position was all over London. He had called for the pleasure of feeling the sensation of my pain bouncing off satellite dishes around the world. I knew that, of course, so there was no way I would give him that satisfaction.

I now had to ponder a bit about where he had gotten his information. Clearly, he thought I was bearish on the pound, and in this case he was right. But it was unusual for my cash positions to correspond to my market views.

At Salomon, Bankers, and Soros, banks would often observe my trades or look at my cash positions and believe that they corresponded to my market views. But often that wasn't the case. Usually my cash positions were hedges against my option views. Sometimes I used my cash positions to put on synthetic option positions, or as a hedge to reduce exposure in a position that I thought would continue the opposite way of my cash position. In other words, just because I was short pounds in spot didn't necessarily mean I was bearish on the pound. In fact, I might have been wildly bullish on the pound—and was simply taking some profits by selling some pounds against an otherwise more dominant option portfolio.

But in this case, the sadistic traders whose calls lit up the switchboard were right: I was bearish on the pound, and I was short. And at the moment, I was being absolutely honest. It *was* a good trade number. I meant what I said: Anyone trading that day should be long pounds.

"Excuse me," I said to my first caller, "there are some other calls coming in. I'll talk to you later."

The switchboard was still dancing with blinking lights. I chose another line at random.

"Hey, mate, how you doin'?" Another chirpy voice. "What're you thinkin'? That was a great number, wasn't it?"

"Yes, that was a great number." Without waiting for him to ask my opinion, I said, "I think you ought to be long pounds today. I think that it's going to go right through the moon. In fact, I think we have a chance today to take out one ninety-one."

An uncomfortable silence followed.

I asked him, "What are you thinking?"

"Oh, I just wanted to check in and see how you're doing."

"I'm doing fine," I said. "Just fine, thanks." When

he didn't comment, I added, "I understand there are some big short positions in the market. Do you think they're going to square up today?"

Stunned silence again. Then, "What do you mean?"

"Well, I understand there are some very large speculative short positions out there. Do you think they're going to get squeezed out?"

From his silence I could sense the confusion and bewilderment. I could almost see the gears spinning in his mind: "Maybe I've got it all wrong. Maybe Andy's really long. No rational person would sit there, short a billion pounds, and talk like that. Is he lying? But he hasn't lied. He hasn't said he's not short. I don't understand this guy. What is he doing?"

Another call. This time the voice was phlegmatic. One of my friends was calling from Singapore. This was the voice of a killer.

"I'm told there are some big shorts around the market in sterling," he said.

"Yeah, that's what I've heard."

"Do you know anything about that?" he pursued.

"You mean you want to know my position?"

Singapore didn't reply.

So I added, "The fact of the matter is that I'm short pounds. I think the pound is at least ten to fifteen percent overvalued. I think it's going to collapse. I think it's going to drop at least twenty cents. I think it's the stupidest boom-bust situation I've seen in the market in five years. It's way overdone. But if you're asking what I think today, I think the pound's bid. I think it's a good number. I think people are going to try buying it. I think they're going to try squeezing me out of my shorts."

"Oh." A pause. "Well, does that mean you're going to go out and try to buy your pounds back?"

"Well, I'm certainly not going to tell you before I do it. But I'm sure you'll know it's happened before it's over. I've got to go. There's another call coming in."

I knew that every trader who called that morning was trying to get a sense of my conviction and my pain. Each of them wondered whether I was going to square up just because of one number—a number that, deep down, I knew was an aberration. I still believed—in fact, I believed with every fiber of my system—that the pound was overvalued and that it was getting ready for a big fall. Still, that conviction didn't stop me from feeling like I had just been attacked by a pack of hungry dogs. I knew all the traders were going to try to push the pound higher, just to see if they could attract some fresh buying.

After the tenth call, I decided to stop answering the telephone. It was starting to get a bit wearying, and I was getting tired of fending off the wolves. My trading partner had never witnessed this kind of behavior before. At the end of these conversations, he turned to me. There was a stunned look on his face.

"Did you have to go through that all the time you were at Bankers?"

"Generally, yes."

"I can't believe it," he said. He still looked white as a sheet.

Of course, he was only partially responsible for our position on this trade. His trading limit was 100 million dollars. The bulk of this position was mine. Still, I'm sure he felt like the copilot on a doomed flight. The way the pound was going, it looked as if we were about to lose both wings and the tail.

"What are you going to do?" he asked.

"Well, I think I'll watch to see if it's real."

I sat back and watched the screen.

My risk, at that point, was largely limited to the premium I'd spent on the options. I had locked in some profits—and the rest were "opportunity costs." But as I watched the numbers on the screen, I kept thinking, "God, I wish I were long."

The pound went up another penny. I saw it spike above $1.90 and keep going.

The adrenaline rush got worse. I tried to remember what had become of the stupendously prescient idea I'd had, not that long ago, that the pound was going to plummet. What had become of the intelligent, self-confident, perspicacious trader who had formed a reasonable, rational conviction that all the market forces were going to push sterling down? Why had I followed Soros's advice? I remembered his last words: "When it starts going your way, really let 'em have it."

Well, I'd let 'em have it.

When I had hedged the options, it had seemed like the right thing to do. Now it seemed like insanity. The other 400 million pounds that I had sold were more of a problem. I had decided to buy them back if the pound rallied past $1.91 as these pounds were not protected by an offsetting option exposure. Still, maybe I had been right. Any moment, the market could turn around. But I had to admit the world had changed since I'd formed my original idea. When I'd begun establishing this huge trade, I hadn't anticipated the condition my psyche would be in today. Right now I was feeling vulnerable. I had been without sleep so long that there was a question of how much longer I could keep my eyes open— but more important, how much longer I wanted to.

I began to feel more comfortable when the pound topped out at the $1.9050 level. That was when I decided to add on one final twist to the position. When the pound dropped under $1.8950, I decided to sell an extra 200 million pounds. The pound was coming off its highs, twenty points at a clip. It came off a bit more until it had dropped nearly a penny. I felt that there was a huge battle being waged. The market was still tenaciously holding on to its pounds. There were traders out there who were convinced that sterling was going to go up to 1.95 or 2.00 against the dollar. And I was convinced that it was going to go the other way—that it would drop about twenty cents.

For a while, I thought I was the only guy in the world who really wanted the pound down. Then the Bank of England stepped in and began selling. I was delighted—and relieved—to have the company of a central bank.

The market reacted sharply to the Bank of England's intervention and continued to sell off. I judged that the traders were already long and that they didn't want to own any more.

I rang up a bank in London. The trader I talked to was one of those who had called earlier that morning to measure the intensity of my pain.

When he picked up the line, I said, "Hey, what's going on with cable?"

"We're seeing some intervention here from the Bank of England," he replied.

I said, "Oh, can I have a price on fifty million pounds, please?"

"Sure."

I knew he would be expecting me to buy back some pounds. But I decided if I was committed to the trade, this was a good level at which to sell a little more, just to see how the market felt.

The London trader came back on the line.

He quoted me a price of 1.8880–85.

I sold him fifty million pounds.

"Huh?" I heard some slow breathing. "Uh—you want to *sell* the pounds?"

"Yes," I said. "At eighty, I want to sell fifty million pounds."

"You're selling the pounds?"

"Yes," I repeated. "At eighty. I'd like to sell fifty million pounds at eighty."

"Oh. At eighty?"

"Yes. At eighty. Fifty million pounds at eighty."

"Okay. Thank you."

"Thank you," I replied, and hung up.

During the next few minutes I called back three more of the other banks that had called me that morning, and I sold my final 150 million pounds.

By then I had supplied the extra 200 million pounds to the market, so my total position was 1.1 billion pounds. I had sold 500 million pounds against the option and 600 million pounds spot. In terms of the whole portfolio, which was $1.8 billion, it wasn't a heavily leveraged position, particularly since only 600 million of the pounds were unhedged. But in terms of the market, it was a big position.

I wondered how the market would respond.

As it turned out, it didn't respond well at all.

The pound fell like a stone. In a very short time it

dropped all the way to $1.8450, six cents from the high. The traders who got caught long that day had gotten sucked into a speculative bubble with no solid support, and the bubble was popping.

As the pound continued to ease, the short-term speculators were forced to unload their long positions. Early the next day, as the pound continued its decline, I decided the suffering and torment I had endured during the past forty-eight hours were sufficient and it was time to take my profits. I quietly purchased 100 million pounds as the price fell, and it was at that point that I placed the order to buy back a billion pounds—an order which I regretted for quite some time. All I really wanted to do was buy back my position, go home, and get some sleep. I didn't want to create an international commotion. I had executed larger trades before, without much reaction, so I assumed the market would digest this short-term shift in the supply-demand function quite smoothly. I could square up and be all done.

I didn't think it would take more than fifty, sixty, or at most seventy points to take in a billion pounds. The market had been extremely liquid, and there were a lot of traders running around with 50-million-pound positions. What I didn't anticipate was that the sterling would move up two full cents as the bank I had selected executed my order, creating a market condition of chaos and panic.

The next day in the papers, there were some stories about my trading. My name had been leaked to the press by people at the bank that had handled my trade. Traditionally, traders assume that banks are supposed to be discreet. Some of the ones I dealt with certainly were not. (Having learned my lesson, I now deal only with banks that maintain the highest degree of professionalism.) Everyone I spoke to knew the size of the order and knew what time it had been placed. I certainly hadn't told anyone in the press. So I knew there were tremendous leaks of proprietary information.

I was upset by the lack of confidentiality. Not only that, but whoever spoke to the press got the story entirely wrong.

Somewhere the rumor had started that the Bank of England was angry because of my heavy buying of sterling. If so, the Bank of England never spoke to me about it—nor to the best of my knowledge did the Old Lady (as B of E is called in international banking circles) ever speak to anyone at Quantum. The truth was, I didn't want sterling to go up. All along, I really wanted the pound to go down. There have been only a few times in my trading career when the central bank and I have both been on the same side. This was one of them. But according to all the rumors that came afterward, the Bank of England was upset because it looked like I was going against it.

I went to bed and slept for 16 hours.

About a week after I had fully liquidated my position, the pound collapsed. I had been right, after all. I had made a $30 million profit, but if I had stayed in another week, I would have made a $100 million profit. On the other hand, it could have been much worse.

One Friday evening several weeks later, I was having dinner with some friends when the phone rang. It was my plumber. About a week before, when he had fixed the toilets and installed a new sink, we had talked a bit about the world. He had been interested in what I was doing. Now he was interrupting my dinner with an urgent call.

"Andy, you're on TV. You're famous," he said. "I knew you could do it!"

"What are you talking about?"

"You're being interviewed on TV," he said.

I thanked him for the information. I hadn't been interviewed for any program, and I had no idea what he was talking about, but I thought I should find out. I went back to the dinner table and excused myself. "I'm sorry, I have to turn on the TV. Apparently I'm being interviewed. I want to know who they dressed up like me to do this interview."

It was Adam Smith's *Money World*, on the subject of "Foreign Currency Traders." Among the guests were John Williamson from the Institute for International

Economics and Stephen H. Axilrod from Nikko Securities. Somewhere the producers had found a photograph of me, which they had blown up and propped up on a pile of pound notes. I wasn't actually saying anything, but on the other hand, I didn't have to: They were saying it all for me—talking about Andy Krieger and the billion-dollar bet . . . and they got it all wrong.

"Krieger's bet," said an announcer (one of those voice-overs that sounds like the Word of Truth on TV), "was that the market forces would push the pound higher, even though the Bank of England was trying to hold it down."

That, of course, was exactly the opposite of what I had been trying to do. From the beginning, I had bet the pound would go down. I had been praying for it to go down while the Bank of England had probably been selling billions of pounds to *push* it down. Where was the conflict in that?

Commenting on the monetary policies of Britain, John Williamson observed, "There was really no other way to fight inflation but to let the exchange rate go through the ceiling . . . so that would have been an invitation to a trader to bet large sums on the assumption that the pound was going to go up."

"Well," said George J. W. Goodman (who calls himself "Adam Smith"), "if he could see this, why didn't you and I see it? I mean, these are the kind of macro events that we both look at, and this seems like a one-way bet."

"Why didn't we see it?" asked Mr. Williamson. "I suppose we weren't focusing on the issue. It wasn't our job to look for those market opportunities."

Mr. Smith: "If I understand you correctly, what he (Andy Krieger) observed was an anomaly that the fiscal policy of Britain didn't match the monetary policy of Britain, is that it?"

Mr. Williamson: "Well, that's my guess as to what lay behind it, yes. It could be that it came at a later stage and was a pure gamble that the pound was going to go on up, because it had been going up, but betting that much money, I would think he probably had something more than that in mind."

He sure did. What he had in mind was covering his short sterling position before he got buried, taking some profits, and going home to bed. I switched off the TV and went back to the table.

"I don't think they got it right," I said.

5

The Dialectics of Decision Making

I SUSPECT THAT, like a lot of other traders, my initial preoccupation was with professional survival, and it was only after I became established that my emphasis shifted to gaining a deeper insight into the market. Yes, the object is making money, but in a different sense, the object is anticipating the market. If I'm going to win consistently at this game, the trader concludes, I have to understand the geography of the mine field. And the foreign-exchange market offers the trader the greatest challenge in the world—a challenge that is, in fact, as large as the world.

What is the decision-making process of a trader? To take the narrow view, I would of course like to believe that my methods, incentives, and approaches are unique. But in reality, many currency traders probably entertain thoughts that are similar to mine, and they make their "buy" and "sell" decisions based on data that is available to all of us. No single trader, of course, determines the value of the currency in your pocket. Rather, hundreds of thousands of traders, making millions of trades every day, finally determine what your dollar is worth against the yen, deutsche mark, pound, and other currencies.

So, to understand how your dollar waxes and wanes in value, perhaps it is worthwhile to look at how one trader makes his decisions.

To define the relevant data, a trader has to be analytical. Take the simple statement that a currency is "bid." Taken at face value, what that means is, "It's going to go up . . . or, at the very least, it doesn't want to go down."

But *why* is it bid? What does that mean?

A currency is bid only when there is an abundance of bids for the currency. In other words, demand for the currency is being shown by a steady, seemingly endless stream of bids. But what sort of demand is it? Is it a result of trade flows or capital flows? Is the currency bid because the fundamentals of that nation's economy are good, or simply because traders have gotten into the habit of bidding for the currency? And what if all the bids are filled in by supply—will there then be additional bids at slightly lower price levels, reflecting deeper levels of demand?

The trader may have some awareness of where the bids are coming from, and if he were to examine that awareness, he might be able to analyze whether the deeper levels of demand actually exist. But sometimes it's better if a trader is *not* aware of all the processes in the market that show up as demand. Given a particular market situation, maybe it's better for the trader if he restricts himself to the simpler view—"It's bid, so I'll buy it." Or, "It's offered . . ." (that is, there is a steady stream of supply shown through offers of the currency) ". . . so I'll sell it."

At every point, the trader has to decide what is actually happening. Sometimes a currency is bid, but it's not going up—so perhaps the supply is more powerful. Sometimes the bids are simply the ill-fated efforts of some speculators who are trying to fight a bearish trend, so the currency is not in fact bid, but is offered. Maybe the currency is bid because there is a short-term shortage in the market and traders are trying to take back their short positions. Or it might be bid because traders want to go long.

A trader is constantly trying to take in all the data and come to some basic conclusions about the pricing issues. He may be asking, "What does the overall supply–demand function look like at this price at this time?

Are we about to break out into a new range? What fundamental economic data are important now?"

Many layers of analysis may be necessary before one can correctly forecast how a currency will react to a series of world events. This process is complicated by the fact that markets often react perversely when significant news breaks, and sometimes the initial reactions are quite wrong.

Suppose, for example, the price of oil skyrockets because of conflict in the Middle East. What will that do to the yen? On the one hand, higher oil prices are bad for Japan because the country is a very large importer of oil. But that also means the Japanese are probably going to raise interest rates significantly to choke off the growing inflationary pressures. Maybe that's good for the yen, because the high interest rates are going to attract investors . . . so what is bad for Japan may be good for the yen.

Conversely, maybe the rise in oil prices is even worse for the dollar than it is for the yen. If the U.S. economy is weak, it will be less able to endure higher interest rates and less flexible in its ability to address the inflationary aspects of the oil price shock. In fact, the United States might even be forced to ease interest rates somewhat to forestall a financial crisis emanating from the weakening of the economy due to the oil price rise. This would exert downward pressure on the dollar as lower interest rates make dollar-denominated assets less attractive, and the dollar would be weakened still further by the unaddressed rise in inflation.

So, when oil prices soar, the trader's initial reaction might be to sell yen. But then he has to ask himself whether that's the wrong reaction. Maybe, in fact, he should be selling dollars.

But wait! Oil imports are invoiced in dollars. So there's going to be demand for extra dollars, because more dollars will have to be purchased to buy the oil.

No—hold on. It's true, the world's oil is invoiced in dollars, but think about the oil the United States imports from OPEC. The cost of that oil runs to $4–$5 billion every month. If OPEC prices were to go up, the American economy would be hit hard. This is going to make our trade deficit worse, and the already weak economy is going to be shattered.

With perfectly good cause and sound reasoning, a trader can probably talk himself into or out of any position.

And then, just when a position makes perfect sense, there's fresh news. Has a finance minister, or a group of ministers, or the secretary of the Treasury made a comment to financial reporters? Or perhaps an unexpected political development has changed the whole scenario. A trader must then analyze what happened the last time someone made a similar comment and the market reacted.

Was there a delayed reaction? If there is now a sudden move, is this a false move based upon rumor? Or a real move—but also based upon the rumor? Perhaps the rumor will become a fact—or is already a fact—and if that's the case, traders are trading on fact instead of rumor. So what should I be doing—trading on a rumor that everyone else believes, or trading on a rumor that will have the force of a fact if everyone believes the rumor?

Sometimes traders sell the rumor and buy the fact. Other times, they buy the rumor and sell the fact. Sometimes traders buy the rumor and buy the fact; or they sell both rumor and fact.

For example, suppose people know a bad U.S. trade number is going to be announced, indicating a larger-than-expected trade-balance deficit, and therefore they sell dollars. Whether or not I believe the trade number is going to be bad, should I also sell dollars? Suppose I think the trade number is going to be better than expected. Should I be selling dollars because of the rumor—or should I go long dollars because I believe the dollar will bounce back when the trade figures are announced?

In addition to considering the relative importance

of actual news and rumors of news, each trader also considers the many internal factors related to the economy. Is there an abundance of land and raw materials? What are the human resources—that is, how well educated and well trained are the people? What is the nation's attitude toward trade-intervention policies? What is its attitude toward a strong or weak currency? (One country might want a strong currency to keep inflation down, while another might want a weak currency to build up exports.)

Political structures also play a role in the trader's decision making. Has one nation elected a conservative government—and, if so, how will that affect its economic system? Has another nation implemented reforms—and, if so, how will those reforms affect its economy and investors' perceptions of that economy?

Often, on balance, the nations and economies are only a background to the foreign-exchange market itself. In order to determine which way the currency is most likely to go, the foreign-exchange trader must have a view on *other* traders' views of the currency. Are they bullish? Are they bearish? Since they're all hooked into Reuters screens, presumably they've all read the same figures and the same news announcements. But they may well interpret those bulletins differently.

Now the trader begins a process of taking the same information that's flowing worldwide and asking: Is there a contrary view that has validity? And, if so, do I (as a trader) have a strong enough conviction to take a position and risk losing some money on that view?

The trader's point of view bears no resemblance to the view of the directors of the central bank of the nation in which his chair, desk, screen, and phone happen to be located. A U.S. trader does not care whether he exchanges yen, deutsche marks, Swiss francs, or Australian dollars, as long as he ends up with profits. (I might add that most companies employing foreign-exchange traders do not have a particular patriotic bias either.)

Of course, any U.S. trader would love to know whether his country's secretary of the Treasury and the Federal Reserve chairman are bullish or bearish on the dollar; but he wants to know only as a trader and an investor, not as a citizen who has a patriotic commitment to his currency.

Traders call one another constantly, sometimes to share their views, sometimes to air their apprehensions, sometimes just because they are confused.

Trader A calls Trader B. "What do you think?" he asks.

"Well," says Trader B, "right now the fundamentals are terrible and the technicals look terrible. I mean, we all know the United States is in a recession, and everyone knows U.S. rates are going lower and overseas economies are booming. But does that mean everyone's already short dollars?"

"I don't know. Maybe."

"Well, if they're already short dollars, maybe we should be buying our shorts back. But we think that, overall, the buck is supposed to go lower. So I'm sitting here short dollars because I think no one else is short. But even if they were short, I'd probably want to be short, except maybe it's going to bounce. So—what am I supposed to do? Should I take profits and sell dollars back out higher, or am I supposed to just stay short and assume it's going to bounce? Maybe it's okay if it bounces—because eventually it's going to go down."

There's a self-questioning dialectic that most traders entertain continuously. The dialectic turns fiercest when the question is whether to take profits. Losses are easy, because some price or loss limit will automatically trigger the liquidation of a position. Profits are tougher, because if I miss profit-taking opportunities by getting out too soon, or I wait too long and the profit turns to a loss, the psychological impact is greater. Traders become attached to their profits *before* they have actually been taken. And there's often an inner monologue about *when* to take profits. That one-sided conversation might go as follows:

The last four times that I didn't take profits when it went my way, I ended up liquidating my position for a loss. So now the question is, since I have a profit, am I supposed to take my profit, or is this the time it's going to follow through and turn into a big trend? After all the suffering I've been through on this trade, it would drive me crazy to miss the big move when it finally comes.

With hindsight, of course, every trader would always do the right thing. He would always know when to cover and when to reestablish at the perfect level.

Proper trading is not gambling. Deciding the size of one's trade, deciding the allowable loss provisions for every idea, and devising a systematic approach to the process of taking profits requires prudent money management and risk management. By designing and following a risk-management system, the trader can relax and focus on the markets because the maximum losses of his portfolio are defined, assured, and tolerable. A risk-management system will further ensure that the psychological and emotional shifts of the trader will not alter the overall risk-reward profile of the entire portfolio.

When traders are feeling emotionally weak and vulnerable, they tend to make the wrong decisions. They tend either to take profits too soon or to give up on their convictions too easily. Conversely, when traders have had a good run and made a lot of money, they tend to become overconfident. When a trader is convinced that his ideas and his decision-making process can't be wrong, he may ride a position too far when it's going against him. He may even end up giving back everything he made from a more successful trading period. The systematization of one's trading methodology vis-à-vis position size, frequency of trades, and profit-and-loss-taking rules will ensure that the portfolio will be properly and consistently managed over time.

To a large degree, every trader is striving to understand a creature inadequately perceived. That creature is the market. It moves restlessly throughout the day and night, responding to the pulse of the world, sometimes shrinking, sometimes swelling. We traders help to determine its course; we feed it; we cajole it; we play with it; but we are also its victims.

Each of us goes through a painful learning process in discovering that the market is beyond our control. We can push the market. We can prod it. One trader, or a mass of traders, can excite it into motion. But ultimately it moves of its own accord; it finds its own way. That is the fascination of it, and ultimately the frustration. The market is always right, and over time no one player can ever hope to dominate it. The foreign-exchange trader must focus on his own positions, his own profits and losses. But what determines those profits and losses is, ultimately, the world and the market forces in motion.

Here's a good example:

On October 19, 1987, the stock market crashed. Currencies remained relatively stable for a while, even the "junk bond" currencies which offered high interest rates and lousy fundamentals. I was convinced that these high-yielding currencies were terribly overvalued, so I began paying close attention to two of them, the Aussie (the Australian dollar) and the kiwi (the New Zealand dollar). I'd had a few nasty experiences with the kiwi, after which I had left it alone.

As I noted that global investors were shifting their assets from high-yielding, speculative plays to more conservative, secure alternatives, I decided to venture another foray into the peculiar world of Australian currencies. I had already earned more than $100 million during the year, and I was willing to invest some of those profits in a large kiwi option position.

I knew that investors had been buying kiwi because it had a high interest rate and the currency had been stable to strong. Therefore the holders of the currency were earning the large interest rate differential between

New Zealand interest rates and U.S. dollar interest rates as well as the price appreciation. As they kept buying kiwi, the currency kept going up. I could see a boom-bust scenario developing. And as I thought about it, I said to myself, "This is a stupid situation. The currency rallied from fifty-four cents to sixty-seven cents, simply because of the interest rates. I don't believe its current price level is justified."

I called up a Kiwi trader, and asked, "What's going on?"

"Mate," said a helpful voice, "there's only one way for this currency to go."

"Oh," I asked, "which way is that?"

"Up," he replied. "There's a CPI [Consumer Price Index] number coming out today. If it comes out higher than expected, it means everyone is going to buy the kiwi because it means higher interest rates. People will be buying to get the high yield. And if it comes out lower than expected, people will buy the kiwi because the fundamentals will look better. They'll all be buying bonds to capture the capital appreciation. So, no matter what happens, people are going to be buying kiwi."

"Wow, that sounds like a pretty easy game. That's really helpful. I'll have to think about that."

I called another trader: "What do you think about the kiwi here?"

"Oh, mate, there's only one way for this currency to

go. It's going to go up. Corporates are all buying, and we understand there are some big players offshore who are all short."

I said, "Oh? This is the first time I heard about that."

He said, "Yeah, apparently Solly's been selling a lot of kiwi. They're really caught. They must be short at least fifty or a hundred million kiwi. They're going to have to cover."

By "Solly," he meant Salomon Brothers, and I had worked there long enough to know they weren't going to cover because of an adverse move on 50 million kiwi. If it went two cents against them, they would lose only a million dollars—not a big problem for Salomon. I was annoyed because the dealer was giving out information that I certainly hadn't asked for and that was none of my business. I thought it was unprofessional. Maybe he was doing it to give me a feel for how much he knew about the market. I wasn't impressed.

I called up another trader. "What's going on?"

He said, "Ah, mate, this kiwi's bid. It's going to go through the moon."

"Why?" I asked.

"These high interest rates are just attracting all these offshore investors. They're all buying." And then he added, "There's one big guy who's short."

"Oh?" I said. "An investment house out of New York?"

"Yep," he said. He added, "They're really short. They must be caught at least fifty to a hundred million short. And we understand the corporates here are going to try to squeeze 'em."

It seemed to me that they were relying too much on the belief that Salomon was short and the market had moved against them. Even though it wasn't hurting me, and there was nothing illegal about it, I was beginning to like their attitude less and less.

So I called up another trader. Same thing. And another. The story was just the same.

After I made the rounds, I thought, "This is stupid. They're all telling me they think there's only one way for it to go." It certainly sounded like a boom-bust to me. And since everyone was buying kiwi, I thought I should probably sell some. I called back the first trader I'd talked to and said, "Can you please make me a price on fifty million kiwi?"

"Oh, yeah, sure, mate. No problem."

The price marked on the screen was around $.6640–50.

"Hold on," he said after a moment. "Price coming. Ticky, ticky, hold on." Then: "Sixty–seventy for you, mate."

"At sixty," I said, "I want to sell fifty million kiwi."

He started clicking the phone. "Hold on. You want to *sell* fifty million kiwi?"

"Yes, at sixty I want to sell fifty million kiwi."

"You want to *sell* the kiwi?"

"Yes, I want to sell fifty—"

"Hold on. I'm sorry, the dealer's changed his price now. The best I can do for you is forty."

"Forty?" I couldn't believe it. In a split second, the price had changed from 60 to 40. I was beginning to admire this trader's professional behavior even less. After what I hoped was a moment's pause, I said, "Okay, at forty I give you fifty million kiwi."

Now I was truly annoyed.

And the screens were getting marked up. The price on the screen went from 40–50 to 50–60 and then 60–70.

It wasn't long before the phone rang. It was a familiar voice.

"Gee, these corporates are really buying," said the voice. "The currency is really bid."

This was just a bit of salt to rub in the wound. I had sold kiwi; now it was going up; clearly, if it continued to go up I could end up losing a nice sum of money.

When the price on the screen was around 80–90, I called the first trader again and asked, "Can I have a price on fifty million kiwi?"

"Yeah, sure, hold on a second." A moment later: "Figure twenty on sixty-seven cents." The screen still showed $.6680–90.

He was quoting me twenty points above the market three-tenths of a percent—a huge amount in currency dealing. Plus, the bid-ask spread was very wide.

"At the figure," I said, "fifty million kiwi yours."

"You want to sell the kiwi?"

"Yes, at the figure."

"You want to sell the kiwi?" he repeated. "I'm sorry, the dealer's changed the price. The best I can do for you is seventy-five."

He'd done it again—changed the price on me after I had dealt.

"At seventy-five," I said, without much warmth. "Fine, I'll give you fifty million kiwi." In a little country with 3 million people and not a big economy, 50 million is a big amount.

I was disgusted. How was I supposed to trade this market? How many times would he come back to me and say, "The dealer's changed the price?"

As I sat watching the prices, Zealand traders were pushing the screens up. It looked as if someone was artificially bidding the currency higher again. But on the other hand, maybe there really was some natural demand for the kiwi.

This went on for a couple of days. I watched the kiwi trading up and down. Finally I called one of my friends, a currency trader at Salomon.

"I'm hearing in the market that you guys are short kiwi," I said.

"Really?"

"Yeah. A number of traders have told me that. Pretty professional, aren't they?"

"Yeah. But I make a lot of money trading kiwi."

"It still bothers me."

"Me too."

"You want to do me a favor?" I asked. "Why don't you get me a price on—oh—a hundred million kiwi. I want to sell some. And since I'm hearing you're short, I'm sure you're going to get a good bid out of them."

"Sure, why not."

He called up a bank in New Zealand and asked for a price on 100 million kiwi. The dealer quoted a price, and my friend sold him a hundred million.

On the screen, the price went down about twenty or thirty points and came right back up.

He said, "My God, I guess it is bid."

I said, "Thanks for the deal."

After I booked my deal with Salomon, I was short 200 million kiwi. Having watched this currency trade around, up and down and back and forth, I began thinking to myself, "This is the stupidest thing I've ever seen. This whole market has been artificially pumped up. There must be a huge number of stops at lower prices."

Since a stop represents a predetermined level at which traders will unload their positions, if the kiwi trades at those stop levels, there is likely to be massive dumping of long positions.

I decided I was willing to invest several million dollars on the trade. I felt this was a market that could easily drop 10 percent. My sources had assured me that the New Zealand government was concerned about an excessively strong kiwi injuring the domestic export business, so I was confident the government would ultimately be on my side. That is to say, I figured that if the kiwi were to fall sharply, the central bank would be unlikely to interfere with its decline; at the very least, it would not come in to push the kiwi higher.

As an intellectual backdrop, I held in constant consideration the instability in the financial markets. With the recent U.S. stock-market crash, and with interest rates at artificially high levels, I realized there would be continued instability. That would lead to further nervousness on the part of investors. Eventually, all the different fund managers around the world who had been buying kiwi for the yield would have to liquidate in a massive global flight to quality.

I called up a dealer in Sydney.

"How's your liquidity down in New Zealand?"

He said, "Oh, pretty good, mate. We'll put some brokers on, get some prices."

"Good. Where is it?"

"Sixty-six fifty sixty."

I said, "Sell fifty million kiwi."

The dealer in Sydney went out and hit the bid. It started going down.

That was interesting. I said to myself, "Well, that's the first time it hasn't gone *up* after I sold it. Since it's going down, I guess I'd better sell some more."

So I called Sydney again and said, "Sell fifty million more."

They sold some more. I had purchased a substantial amount of call options and I was simply selling spot kiwi against my outstanding option exposure. I had been slowly establishing the short-currency position, but when the market started to break down more quickly, I accelerated my selling in order to finish putting on my hedge. After a few hours of steady selling, I had nearly completed my business, and the market reaction reflected my view that the currency was on its way to much lower levels. By the end of the evening, the kiwi had dropped all the way to the .625 level as massive stop losses poured in from all over the world. The lower the currency dropped, the greater the supply in the market. So much for standard economic theories of supply and demand. I decided to wait for the market to bounce back a bit before completing my selling, so after the kiwi rallied to .645 I put on my final hedge. The currency was basically headed lower, and I was perfectly positioned.

Several days later, after the market finished dumping its kiwi positions, the currency finally found some reasonable demand around the .59 level. The confident words that kept running through my head were those of the first trader: "Mate, there's only one way for this currency to go—up." That may have been what he and every other kiwi trader truly believed. No doubt, it was what they all wanted to believe. But it wasn't true. It's never true. In an open market, there are always two ways a price can go—up and down.

I suspect that a lot of people lost a great deal of money on this play. Banks, corporations, and investment houses were taking positions based upon the completely irrational and fundamentally implausible assumption that this currency could only go up. Ultimately, there was a lack of sufficient demand to hold the currency up—and when it started to collapse, it went farther than anyone had anticipated.

During the kiwi move, I was obliged to attend a morning meeting at Bankers Trust. I rarely went to meetings, which usually contributed less to the bank's profitability than following the screens did. But this particular morning, I knew the attendees would be discussing my positions—if they knew what they were. I had not yet covered all the kiwi that I had sold, and I did not want to discuss it. The key people in Bankers' management knew my exposures, and that was sufficient. I preferred to keep my positions discreet.

Customarily, all the spot trades showed up in Bankers' New Zealand "Nostro" account—a check-clearing house for foreign-currency trades located in Wellington. Since I didn't want my spot position broadcast, I rolled it out into the forward market. With all the positions swapped out, the people outside the Bankers system wouldn't know whether I was long or short, whether I was looking for the kiwi to go up or down. All they would see was massive activity. In fact, I had actually swapped more kiwi than I was short out to the different forward markets. It caused an impact in the forward markets, but the net result was that no one outside the system actually knew what my position was.

Prior to the meeting, I had heard one rumor that Andy Krieger was short as much as 200 million kiwi. This was considered an enormous risk. So it was unlikely that anyone would be pleased that I was actually short quite a few times that amount. (Remember, my superiors knew that I had followed my standard practices and purchased Kiwi call options which limited my potential losses to this option premium, which I had already paid.) With a lot more trading immediately ahead of me, I didn't want to be cornered into making long explanations about why I thought the risk was reasonable, justified, and ultimately profitable for the bank.

At the meeting, a number of directors and traders were sitting around talking about what had happened overnight in this or that currency. The Bankers Trust economist was listening in, but like me, he wasn't saying much. Finally, one of the traders turned to me and asked point-blank, "Andy, how big is your short position in kiwi?"

I looked around. My immediate superior was there, and he knew exactly what the answer was. A couple of other traders were trying to look uninterested.

Rather than answer the trader's question directly, I turned to the economist and asked: "I was wondering—how large is the money supply in New Zealand?"

The question was followed by an awkward silence.

A few moments later, the meeting was dismissed. We all left the room, and I went back to trading.

6

Bretton Woods and
All That

WHAT CREATED this market? How did the nations of
the world conclude that international currency exchange
should be determined by profit-oriented traders sitting
in front of computer screens with telephones glued to
their ears?

The truth is that the mandate for the foreign-
exchange market was simply the by-product of economic
necessity. To understand the genesis of this market, one
needs to look back about five decades, to the first meeting of the International Monetary and Financial Conference of the United and Associated Nations. The meeting
was held in Bretton Woods, New Hampshire, in July
1944, one month after the invasion of Normandy.

Europe was in ruins. The end of the war was in sight,
but after the end there would have to be rebuilding, and

rebuilding would cost money. The United States was about to become the postwar financier. America alone, of all the Western nations, had an intact economy, with all factories still running. It had the strongest currency. Business was booming. All the financial ministers who assembled at Bretton Woods recognized that if Europe was going to get on its feet again, the United States would have to lend or give away a huge proportion of its cash reserves.

To set the economic machine into motion after the devastation of the war, the international currency system had to be restructured. Everyone feared rampant inflation—the kind that had crippled Germany after the First World War. In 1916 Germany's currency had been worth about 4 marks to the dollar. By 1923 the official exchange rate was 4 *trillion* marks to the dollar. German citizens pushed wheelbarrows full of cash to the store to buy a few loaves of bread. Between the printing press and the post office window, newly issued stamps had to be overprinted with higher prices. A fundamentally powerful economy devastated by war, Weimar Germany had been gutted by war reparations and staggered by inflation.

From the depths of Germany's demoralization, Hitler and Fascism had emerged. Now that the Second World War had been fought to defeat the Nazis, what would be the rules of the new game? How was someone in the brave new postwar world going to measure the price of a dollar, a mark, a franc? Or a ruble for that matter? Some system had to be found.

The Bretton Woods agenda was to find that system.

Before 1944 most currencies, with the major exception of the pound, were backed by gold. Since one ounce of gold was worth thirty-five U.S. dollars, one dollar was "backed" by exactly 1/35th of an ounce of gold. Each nation's currency was on a "parity" with other currencies, using gold as the measuring stick. The world's gold supply was relatively stable. A certain fixed amount emerged from the earth every year, sweated and toiled for by underpaid miners who never seemed to produce a great deal more or a great deal less. Gold was imperishable. It didn't rust. It didn't get moldy. And as long as currencies were fixed to the gold standard, the world's money supply looked stable. In theory, at least, the United States had enough gold reserves to "back up" all the dollars that could ever be spread around the world. But only in theory.

In 1933, in the midst of the Depression, President Franklin Roosevelt had canceled the dollars-for-gold agreement with U.S. citizens. After that, it was no longer possible, even theoretically, for John Smith to ring the doorbell at Fort Knox and exchange his thirty-five dollars for an ounce of gold. Roosevelt reasoned that if the American economy was going to emerge from the

Depression, it needed to expand. And it couldn't expand with sufficient velocity if paper was still anchored to gold.

Even though the United States went off the gold standard domestically, in the foreign-exchange arena gold was still the unit of measure. Any country that had a balance of payments in its favor could "cash in" its paper dollars for gold bricks. In 1944 American assets were so enormous that it appeared this country would always be a creditor. For the foreseeable future the gold reserves held at Fort Knox and in the vaults of the Federal Reserve Bank of New York would stay there.

As for the domestic wartime American economy, the dollar was inflated, but no one was too concerned. War always brought inflation. The United States had to print dollars to pay the troops and keep the factories running, the trucks rolling, the planes flying. Enormous loans, backed by war bonds, had been extended, but those would be repaid later, with interest. After the war, it was thought, everything would settle down again.

In fact, the earliest paper money was created in similar circumstances. In the mid-1200s, when Genghis Khan had to pay his Mongolian troops to invade North China, he printed military money. After seeing this money, Marco Polo reported: "All these pieces of paper are issued with as much solemnity and authority as if they were pure gold or silver."

After the invasion failed, Genghis Khan's troops were left holding fistfuls of worthless paper. It's a lesson we keep relearning. A currency has value only to the degree that everyone who trades in it agrees to recognize its value. As soon as it becomes impossible (for whatever reason) to trade that currency for something else (gold, silver, commodities, services, or other currency), it becomes worthless. That was the lesson demonstrated by the German currency collapse of 1923—and a lesson well understood by all the ministers who attended Bretton Woods.

Bretton Woods is a shady grove on one side of Mount Washington in New Hampshire, a vacation spot serviced in the 1940s by half a dozen railway lines. More than 730 delegates came to the Mount Washington Hotel. But there was one delegate for whom Bretton Woods was a dream come true. His name was John Maynard Keynes. In 1944 he was sixty-one and in poor health. He had already suffered a number of heart attacks. But he was still at the prime of his intellectual powers. He had always imagined the world's leaders coming together for a rational powwow, to work out a sane global economic system. As Keynes saw it, the world's economic troubles were vast and onerous, but curable.

Keynes was a visionary British economist with the experience of a politician and the instincts of a trader.

Widely respected in academic circles, often consulted by his own government in matters of economics, Keynes had a knowledge of markets that had come firsthand from his own dabbling in the stock exchange. From 1905, when he had bought his first four shares of the Marine Insurance Company for £16, 16s., his investments had grown steadily. (By 1914, his stock assets had been around £14,453, more than four times his annual earnings in academia.)

Keynes had been a firsthand witness to the tragic consequences of the 1919 Paris talks that had resulted in the intensely disputed Treaty of Versailles. France and England, with the acquiescence of the United States, had demanded an intolerable sum of war reparations from Germany and Austria. Keynes had foreseen that the conquered nations of central Europe would be stripped bare. He had also foreseen that the humiliation of the conquered nations would sow the seeds of future bitterness.

In Keynes's view, France and Great Britain depended to a larger degree than they realized (or were willing to admit) on the prosperity of central Europe. If Germany and Austria were plundered, neither nation would have sufficient capital to rebuild its bombed-out factories, repair its transportation network, restart its mines, or purchase the machinery needed to manufacture goods that were required throughout Europe.

At the end of the First World War, Keynes had been

sent to represent the British Treasury at the Peace Conference. He had resigned in protest shortly after firing off a letter to Austen Chamberlain, the chancellor of the exchequer. "The prime minister," Keynes had warned, "is leading us all into a morass of destruction. The settlement which he is preparing for Europe disrupts it economically and must depopulate it by millions of persons."

Immediately after resigning, Keynes had begun work on *The Economic Consequences of the Peace,* his first book. As Germany wallowed in debt, overwhelmed by wholesale inflation, the signatories to the Treaty of Versailles had peered at news photos of desperate Berliners pushing wheelbarrows full of cash along cobblestone streets. Keynes's warnings seemed prophetic: his book had become a best-seller.

Most prophetic of all were his references to the "debauch of the currency" that Lenin too had predicted. Keynes also foresaw that such a debauch could eventually lead to the downfall of capitalist nations. He envisioned a Europe that would be inefficient, weighted with unemployment, and hopelessly disorganized; in Keynes's words, that Europe would be "torn by internal strife, fighting, starving, pillaging, and lying."

The Economic Consequences of the Peace was often shrill, but remarkably prescient. Subsequent events were to prove that Keynes's predictions were largely accurate.

Many of its phrases would haunt the world's leaders in the years to come, particularly Keynes's view that a second war would inevitably arise from the backwash of the first, a direct consequence of the ugly war reparations treaty. "Nothing," wrote Keynes, "can delay for very long that final civil war between the forces of reaction and the despairing convulsions of revolution, before which the horrors of the late German war will fade into nothing, and which will destroy whoever is the victor, the civilization and progress of our generation."

When Keynes met with the leaders of Europe and America at Bretton Woods, the world was in the midst of the war that he had predicted more than twenty years previously. His stature, among this gathering of men with long lives and good memories, was assured.

A stable world required stable economies. The U.S. stock-market collapse of 1929 and the ensuing Depression had created a worldwide ripple effect. Keynes's thesis that all economies were interdependent had been proven beyond doubt. No nation could remain an island of stability if its major trading partners had fundamentally unstable economies. What the world needed, in his view, were a few essentials. First, Western currencies had to be weaned from the great god gold. The restrictiveness of the gold supply meant there would always be limits to the world's currency flows. Gold was fine for a nonexpanding economy that always produced the same quantity of wheat, exported the same number of machine-forged hammers, and bought the same number of oranges every year. But it was no good for an expanding industrial economy in which productivity increased annually and the ratio of imports to exports was constantly shifting.

For such dynamic economies, Keynes argued it was necessary to find something other than gold to use as a standard measure. In his second book, *Tract on Monetary Reform*, published in 1923, Keynes had urged both the United States and Great Britain to go off the gold standard. He advocated that the United States "aim at the stability of the commodity value of the dollar rather than at the stability of the gold value of the dollar." In other words, pin the dollar to importable and exportable goods, rather than to heavy yellow bricks.

The second problem was how to help out nations during their lean years. Inevitably, even the healthiest of economies occasionally encounters bad times. Keynes knew this firsthand: in 1944, with a Depression followed by bombs, Britain was going through the worst of bad times. All of Western Europe was a wreck. Every nation needed assistance. Unless provisions were made quickly, there would be a long, slow, horrendous struggle, as each nation gathered together the shreds of its diminished resources, tried to restore the food chain, rebuilt its homes and factories, and painstakingly created a new economy from the wreckage of the old.

What were the alternatives?

One was a direct handout. Europe needed America's help—there was no way around it. Certainly, the Allies would need massive aid from America. When the long war was over, Germany and Japan would need assistance along with the rest. Europe could rebuild if the United States provided direct aid to the war-torn and crippled nations.

But there was another alternative strongly favored by Keynes—a global lending organization, an international bank that would be financed by countries that had wealth to spare. This bank would lend to the poor and destabilized to help them forge their plowshares and sow their fields. When they rallied, they would not only pay back their loans but also contribute to the global kitty.

If Keynes's dream of a world lending organization were approved at Bretton Woods, wealthier nations would lend to the poorer. With ready access to loans to recapitalize and rebuild, bereft nations would recover quickly from the most devastating war in history. The global economy would benefit.

There was an additional benefit to Keynes's international bank plan. If a central lending organization existed, it would have the power to set currency rates. Keynes suggested a single international currency—

which he called a *bancor*—that would become the standard measure of all other currencies. All the nations that were represented on the board of directors of this lending organization would survey the various economies, discuss rates, and then set a value for each currency relative to the bancor. So the global directors in their collective wisdom might decide that one bancor equaled (hypothetically) 1.50 U.S. dollars, 1 British pound, and 7.5 French francs. As long as the exchange rate was set at those prices relative to the bancor, the rate would be .67 British pounds to the dollar and 5 French francs to the dollar. Trading back and forth among themselves, the nations having a standard reference in the bancor would always know exactly where they stood relative to one another's currencies. Essentially, the bancor would replace gold. But unlike gold, which was limited in supply, the bancor supply would expand to keep up with the burgeoning wealth and productivity of the world's expanding economies.

Even in his most visionary moments, Keynes did not imagine traders, tourists, or corporate chiefs traveling the world with bancors in their pockets. Each nation would still have its own currency that would be used for travel, trade, and international contracts. But each currency would be pegged to the common standard, and that standard would be independent from bullion. The world's economies could expand at their own hectic pace, with some fine tuning along the way, without having their ankles weighted with gold.

There was a convenient discipline in this system. In theory, if one nation's currency became wildly inflated, the directors of the world lending organization would reconsider the monetary situation and exchange ratios. They might suggest to the leaders of nation X, the country with the inflating currency, that they undertake certain controls . . . *or else*. The controls, in this case, would be such things as reducing the money supply by raising interest rates; increasing exports to increase reserves; raising production to lower the cost of goods; or all three. The *or else* part of the equation—and this is where the discipline came in—would be threatening nation X with the devaluation of its currency relative to the bancor. That meant the country would have less international buying power—a slap on the wrist to a nation that needed imports to survive in an interdependent world.

7

Genghis Khan's Dilemma

A FEW MONTHS before Bretton Woods, Keynes met with U.S. Treasury Secretary Harry Dexter White to hash things out. As representatives of different nations, Keynes and White had markedly different agendas. Keynes was fighting for the recovery of the British economy at a time when the United Kingdom had dwindled from a world power into an impoverished and indebted country. By contrast, White flexed the muscle of a credi-tor nation. It was the United States, after all, that would be the lender after the war ended. Like most lenders, it would ultimately decide the terms.

Most of the compromises that came out of those early talks were later approved at the Bretton Woods conference. What emerged was a somewhat out-of-focus version of Keynes's dream. Yes, there would be a world lending organization. It would be named the International Bank for Reconstruction and Development—more simply called the World Bank. And there would be an International Monetary Fund (IMF). The World Bank would borrow from the rich and lend to the poor. The IMF, closely allied to the workings of the World Bank, would have a pool of funds presided over by a board of governors, to make currency adjustments. As Keynes knew, the bank was really a fund, and the fund a bank. By giving all countries access to a pool of international currencies, exchange rates could be stabilized, and nations could receive lines of credit to help them expand their economies.

In the past, whenever a country's imports had exceeded exports, the resulting balance-of-payments deficit had resulted in a tightening of the debtor nation's economy. In an effort to reduce the claims against it, the debtor nation would impose austerity measures, raise interest rates, and tighten fiscal and monetary restraints in order to reduce imports. But, at the same time, debtor nations had to increase production and expand growth in order to make their exports more attractive. The result was the winding down of an economy. Unemployment rose, capital expenditures decreased—the economy went into stagnation.

The purpose of the Bretton Woods program was to give debtors an opportunity to continue smooth growth without sudden contraction when balance-of-payments deficits went up. The dynamics went like this: Assume cherry harvesting was a profitable business for Country Bountiful—and cherries were a hot export item. If Bountiful were paying one million farthings to import magnetos for its mechanized cherry harvesters and only receiving a half-million farthings for the cherries it exported, it could now borrow the additional half-million from its central bank to make up the shortfall. The central bank, in turn, would make up the half-million by borrowing from the International Monetary Fund. Theoretically, this would allow the country to continue buying magnetos for its cherry harvesters; more tons of cherries could be picked and exported; and as income rose from exports, the central bank would pay back its loan to the IMF (along with a small amount of interest).

The net effect, if all went well, was stabilization of Country Bountiful's currency. If its currency started to fall, the central bank would draw on its line of credit at the IMF. It would buy up the currency to keep it within 1 percent of an agreed-upon value. If the balance-of-payments problem got out of hand and the country could not in good faith contemplate further borrowings from the IMF, there was an out. One time only, the nation would be allowed to devalue its currency by as much as 10 percent relative to gold or other currencies.

Although plans for the World Bank and the IMF

were formulated at Bretton Woods, the bancor idea was not accepted. Instead, White proposed, and the Bretton Woods delegates agreed in principle, that the international fund would consist of gold and a mixed assortment of currencies.

Meanwhile, the dollar and most other currencies were still pegged to gold. According to the Bretton Woods agreements, these currencies would be allowed to fluctuate by a certain percentage. In case of dire emergencies, ministers could meet to decide on a one-time rate adjustment for a country that was under severe pressure. But basically the currencies were stabilized at certain fixed values. The bancor was shelved.

When Keynes gave his final speech at the Mount Washington Hotel, he received a standing ovation. As he strode to the door, all 730 delegates sang "For He's a Jolly Good Fellow." No one at Bretton Woods imagined that currency exchange would turn into the anarchy of an open market where currencies were free to float or sink. Only President Richard M. Nixon and his treasurer from Texas had the global vision to make such a nightmare come true—some thirty-five years later.

Neither Keynes nor White would live to see the rebuilding of the war-stricken countries. The two men met once more in Savannah, Georgia, to finalize the details of the Bretton Woods agreements. A year later, on April 21,

1946, Keynes suffered a fatal heart attack. In August 1948, Harry White was forced to defend himself before the House Un-American Activities Committee on charges of supporting Communism—a rather peculiar charge against someone who had just helped set the international capitalist system back on its feet. Within the year, he too was dead, also from a heart attack.

The system Keynes and White had masterminded remained stable for nearly twenty years. Europe recovered. Germany and Japan were rebuilt. Once the Marshall Plan supplied the massive funds needed to restart the engine, the Bretton Woods monetary system began to operate efficiently. The dollar became the world's key currency. With some fluctuations, currencies were generally stabilized; inflation was under control; economies had the means to expand. As John Kenneth Galbraith reflected some years later, "The twenty years from 1948 through 1967 may well be celebrated by historians as the most benign era in the history of the industrial economy."

During that period, however, dollars were flowing into the United States as foreign nations paid for American-made goods. American wealth helped to build NATO defenses as well as rebuild Europe's economy. Dollars were the favored currency—in fact, *the* currency of international exchange. As other economies improved, the United States began importing more goods from countries that had been exclusively buyers. By the mid-1960s the United States was still a net creditor, but its reserves were diminishing.

Then came Vietnam. Among its many devastations, Vietnam managed to help wreak havoc on America's balance of payments. In the jungles of Vietnam—long before the invasion of the products of that fearsome competitor, Japan—the United States began to turn into a debtor nation. That shift had a direct bearing on the foreign exchange.

The keepers of the currency took another hard look at gold. It was fine to have a gold-backed currency as long as nations were (a) in equilibrium in their balance of payments; or (b) willing to take IOUs instead of gold when there were temporary imbalances in payments between countries. But not every nation was satisfied with IOUs. Some wanted gold. And the nation they wanted it from, most of all, was the United States.

In 1950 the United States had $23 billion worth of gold reserves. By 1970 those reserves had dwindled to $11 billion. France was especially eager to hoard. The United States now owed billions of dollars' worth of gold to West Germany, to Britain, to Switzerland—but above all, to France.

Meanwhile, the U.S. currency held by foreign nations increased from $8 billion—where it had been in 1950— to about $47 billion by 1970. Clearly, if all the dollar holders cashed in their dollars for gold, the vaults would be emptied.

It was the weakness Keynes had foreseen, the fatal flaw was gold. The money supply had exploded, and the bullion supply had not. And now, with Vietnam grinding on, soldiers had to be paid and planes had to be built, and dollars were pouring out of the country faster than ever. It was the dilemma of Genghis Khan all over again. Except that the United States, unlike the Mongols, wouldn't let its printed paper turn worthless.

There were only a few ways to stop the weakening of the dollar. Putting an end to the Vietnam War would certainly help. The dollar would also reap some benefits if European nations took on more of the NATO defense burden. And there were other ways: protective tariffs could be imposed, for instance.

In the end, the United States resorted to the alternative that had always been a specter in foreign-currency dealings: it abolished the gold standard.

The events of 1971 essentially created the foreign-exchange market as we know it today. However, the political and economic events leading up to the Nixon administration's actions were exceedingly complex. Much of the action took place behind the scenes—in the heavily carpeted executive offices of central banks; in noisy trading rooms in Geneva, London, and Frankfurt;

at the country estates and state offices of the world's leaders. But the decisions made and the agreements reached would soon have an impact on the world economy and on the lives of the citizens of every nation.

A number of interrelated factors contributed to America's balance-of-payments deficit—and hence the already mounting pressure on the United States to go off the gold standard increased. The most pressing issue was the uncontrolled explosion of Euromoney—above all, the Eurodollar.

Eurodollars were created by bankers from Britain and Western Europe when they began lending dollars across international borders. Until 1950, European banks loaned money to their customers exclusively in the national currency. For example, England loaned British pounds to citizens and corporations in the United Kingdom. French banks loaned French francs to French citizens and businesses. German banks loaned deutsche marks to Germans; and so on. Before Euromoney days, when transactions crossed national boundaries, the receiving bank would accept foreign currency but didn't lend it out again. A French bank that dealt internationally would accept German marks or U.S. dollars, but it wouldn't be in the business of making mark loans or dollar loans to French citizens. Instead, the marks or dollars sat in separate accounts. If the French bank wanted to "settle up" with its German or American counterparts, it could send marks back to Germany in exchange for French francs held in the German bank, or dollars back to the United States in exchange for the francs held in U.S. banks. If these swaps didn't balance out—if there were a continuing deficit on one side of a national border and a "credit account" on the other side—then the ultimate form of settlement was in gold. In 1960, for instance, if France as a nation had a balance-of-payments surplus with the United States and Germany, it had the right to swap its excess dollars for a fixed amount of U.S.-held gold and its excess marks for German-held gold.

It was probably the Soviet Union that first began to change the rules of this particular game. According to Ray Vicker, *The Wall Street Journal's* correspondent in England, the boom in the Eurodollar market was begun quietly by the Moscow Narodny Bank in London. In his book *Those Swiss Money Men*, published in 1973, he described the progression of events: In order to carry on international trade after the Second World War, Soviet bankers had been using dollars instead of rubles. Since the postwar Soviet Union needed all sorts of foreign commodities, it maintained a large balance of hard currency. The strongest or hardest of all currencies at the time was the dollar. The Narodny Bank had become a warehouse for dollars owned by Moscow. Some of these dollars were profits from the few Soviet goods shipped elsewhere, while others had been received in trade for Moscow's gold. Held in the Narodny Bank, the dollars remained idle until such time as they were paid out to foreign suppliers in payment for goods bought by the Soviet Union.

Idle dollars, however, earn no interest, and Soviet bankers, like bankers everywhere, abhor money that sits idle. The Eurodollar market was probably born of Soviet bankers' frustration with idle capital. Under normal circumstances, the Soviets would have invested their dollars in the New York markets. But with the Cold War getting chillier every minute, they were concerned that in the event of political or military strife, Soviet dollar assets held in the United States would be seized by Washington. (This was a valid concern, as history has shown. When the Iranians took American hostages in Tehran, the prompt U.S. reaction was to put a freeze on Iranian assets in the United States.) Given these limitations, the Soviet bankers wondered, why not lend dollars to Europeans—and to Americans operating in Europe—at attractive interest rates?

The timing was perfect. American corporations were rapidly expanding throughout Britain and the rest of Western Europe. Dollars were in demand. If a multinational corporation could borrow dollars at very low interest rates in Europe, why continue shopping at banks in the continental United States? After all, dollars were dollars. According to Vicker, "the first borrowers of these dollars were U.S. corporations which were expanding their manufacturing facilities in Europe." Soon the idea of lending dollars caught on with most of the larger European banks. By 1959 the Eurodollar market had $1 billion in circulation; by 1973 the sum of U.S. dollars sloshing around in the Euromarket was about $80 billion. By 1977 the Eurodollar market would amount to some $380 billion.

All these dollars, however, were cut loose from the control of U.S. monetary authorities. Unlike U.S. banks, which have certain reserve requirements, Eurobanks in most countries are not subject to reserve regulations and interest-rate ceilings. So the dollar-denominated deposits in those banks could flow unrestricted into the European market. The Eurodollars were exchanged among foreign banks and cycled through the central banks without ever reaching U.S. shores.

It wasn't long, however, before U.S. banks caught on and started playing catch-up. One way was to open a "captive bank" in Europe or an "offshore branch" somewhere such as in Bermuda or the Bahamas, where deposits were not subject to U.S. banking regulations.

The mushrooming of Eurodollars had dire consequences for the U.S. balance of payments. Though the dollars were entirely loaned, invested, and used overseas, they were still U.S. dollars—which meant U.S. gold supposedly "backed" that expanding money supply. If a French bank lent a million dollars at 10 percent and got back $1,100,000 by the end of the year, then the United States owed that bank an additional $100,000 worth of gold.

The central banks of most European countries—that is, the banks run by the governments, ostensibly to control currency flows and monetary practices—did little to discourage these practices. The central bankers were perfectly willing to lend Eurodollars to commercial banks and collect dollar interest on the loans. With such massive lending, the Eurodollar market exploded.

American multinational corporations snatched up the excess bargain-rate dollars. In 1968 U.S. customers borrowed $6 billion through European branches; a year later, that figure was $15 billion. A report issued by the German Bundesbank in 1971, reviewing 1970, stated that "central banks invested a fairly large amount of dollar reserves not in the United States but directly or indirectly in the Euromoney market, from where they flowed back to the central banks via the commercial banks of the countries involved; thus the same sum of dollars was added to the monetary reserves several times over."

Meanwhile, U.S. companies and U.S. investors exploited the foreign sources of capital. In December 1971 the chairman of Dow Chemical lavished praise on the generous funding that had been heaped upon so many corporations during that era. In his address to the Business Financing Conference in New York City, he announced, "This pool of expatriate dollars has furnished the world with the one largest capital market available to finance a large part of both private and public capital expansion."

In the process, however, the combination of the balance-of-payments deficit and the expanding Eurodollar market was creating unbearable pressure on the dollar. Although technically it was still pegged to gold and still worth $35 an ounce, that "gold standard" bore no resemblance to market reality. The dollar supply had expanded—America's hoard in gold reserves had shrunk precipitously.

For a time there seemed to be tacit agreement among most foreign nations that they would not initiate a run on the U.S. Treasury reserves. As long as the dollar was sound, they had no reason to swap their dollars for gold. But what if the U.S. gold reserves fell below an "acceptable" level? Would there be a "run on the bank" (in international terms) followed by a massive flight from the dollar?

At the end of 1970 the U.S. balance of payments deficit was $9.8 billion on an official settlements basis. Total claims against the dollar—which were many times larger than the "official settlements" figure—were three times greater than the gold reserves.

Dollars continued to pour out of the United States. Some of those dollars were paid out by U.S. multinationals repaying Eurodollar loans taken out during the preceding years. Some of the money was moved overseas in search of higher returns on investment. By the end of March 1971, when three-month U.S. Treasury bills were paying 3.3 percent, the three-month Eurodollar rate was 5.25 percent, and the three-month interest rate in West Germany was 7.5 percent. Meanwhile, the United States was in the throes of a recession, and banks were *cutting* their lending rates to stimulate growth.

In order to take advantage of high interest rates in these countries, bankers, dealers, and investors around the world began to make Eurodollar deposits. The money that flowed into these countries in search of high returns came to be known as "hot money." Although this hot money was primarily capital in search of a high return on investment, the effect of these capital flows was to shift the balance-of-payments ledger in favor of European nations that had especially attractive rates. As capital left the United States, the flight of investment dollars seriously damaged the U.S. balance of payments.

Dollars poured into Germany, Switzerland, and Great Britain—but especially Germany. Between December 1969 and March 1971, the reserves of gold and foreign exchange in Germany's central bank, the Bundesbank, approximately doubled from under $8 billion to more than $15 billion. Because dollars were leaving the United States, the first quarter balance-of-payments deficit in the United States for 1971 was $5 billion, about four times as large as U.S. Treasury officials had anticipated.

Investors were selling the U.S. dollar. Had the currency market been as unrestricted as it is today, the dollar's value would have plummeted simply because there was little demand for the greenback. But under the Bretton Woods agreements, the dollar was still "pegged" to other currencies. It had certain defined limits or parities above which, and below which, it was not supposed to be traded. For instance, at that time the parity was 3.66 deutsche marks to the dollar, with an upper range of 3.69 and a lower limit of 3.63.

However, in a volatile market the artificially fixed prices became impossible to maintain. How could the central banks continue to hold the dollar to a range between 3.63 and 3.69 deutsche marks when there was a gross oversupply of dollars and a greater-than-ever demand for deutsche marks? The Bundesbank made a valiant attempt to hold the deutsche mark to the agreed-upon peg, but it could do so only by spending massive amounts of its reserves to buy dollars with marks. In effect, this was an artificial way to create a shortage of dollars and generate demand when there was little in the market. By creating a temporary "oversupply" of marks, the Bundesbank hoped to depress the value of the German currency, thereby holding it to the level at which the currency had been pegged.

In the short term, the Bundesbank action had the desired effect. But how long could the central bank continue to sweep up dollars by spending its reserves? If the dollars just kept pouring in, eventually the Bundesbank's reserves would be depleted to critical levels.

In Europe during the week of May 3, 1971, the Bretton Woods agreement entered its death throes. In the United States, the Treasury Department had made some feeble attempts to stem the flow of dollars—but the basic policy of Nixon administration officials was one of "benign neglect." The currency problem was regarded as Europe's problem. At home in the United States, the goal was to stimulate the economy by whatever means possible. But the European central banks couldn't continue buying up U.S. dollars just to keep the price of dollars artificially high. At the end of the business day on Monday, May 3, a report was issued by five influential West German economic institutes. Four of the institutes recommended that West Germany float the mark immediately.

When a currency "floats," it means that its value is

no longer pegged to a particular range of parities with other currencies. The floating currency is essentially up for auction—and the buy-sell activities of traders in the market determine its value.

Remember that under the parities established at Bretton Woods, the mark had a range of 3.63–3.69 against the dollar; if it floated, its range was potentially unlimited. If there was great demand for the mark—as there certainly was at the time—it would literally be "bid" upward if it floated. Of course, when the level got too high, there would be more sellers than buyers and its value would fall. In other words, the West German economic institutes that recommended the float were encouraging a free and open market for the deutsche mark—of the kind we have today.

After these recommendations were released, a wave of speculation followed. Although the mark had not yet gone into an official float, investors anticipated that it would, and they also anticipated that its value would soar as soon as that happened. So they bought in anticipation of a bull market.

On May 4 investors began a wholesale purchase of the deutsche mark. More than a billion U.S. dollars poured into the Bundesbank. On Wednesday, May 5, the Bundesbank accepted $1 billion in the first fifty-five minutes of trading. It took in more than 8 percent of the total U.S. gold and foreign-exchange reserves in less than one hour. Then, at 10:30 A.M. the Bundesbank closed its doors. By 11:00 A.M. the money markets in Zurich had closed down.

In New York, the following day, the Federal Reserve spent about $1 billion to buy government Treasury bills that had been dumped on the market by panicked investors. On Thursday, May 6, Treasury Secretary John Connally made a few brief remarks during a press conference. His Texas drawl was heard around the world. Acknowledging that the money markets in Europe were indeed experiencing a time of stress, Connally announced that there would be no change in U.S. policies. The problem, he said, "can't be attributed to any action of the United States, or to a weakness of the dollar." Three months later, the U.S. government, without congressional approval and in violation of Section 5 of the Bretton Woods Agreement Act, went off the gold standard.

8

All That Glitters Is Not Gold

APPOINTED TO THE POST of secretary of the Treasury in late 1970, John Connally was sworn in on February 11, 1971. Connally was a completely political creature. A tall, energetic Texan of the grass-roots school, he had learned his politics at the right hand of Lyndon B. Johnson and had adopted some of the style and mannerisms of his political mentor. His warmth and charm could send political contributors reaching for their wallets. Nixon had spotted Connally as the right man to acquire the mantle of the presidency after Nixon's second term.

Although Connally's monetary policy was not clear when he took over the Treasury, he began sitting in on meetings run by Treasury Undersecretary for Monetary Affairs Paul A. Volcker—head of the so-called "Volcker Group" within the Treasury. Volcker warned Connally that a devaluation of the dollar was to be anticipated, and Connally took him at his word.

During his early months in office, Connally had few dealings with the State Department. At first, Secretary of State Henry Kissinger only observed Connally from afar, with reserved admiration for Connally's political strength and his direct access to Nixon. Ultimately, the decisions that Connally made about currency matters would have an impact on all aspects of international affairs, and Kissinger's dealings with the secretary of the Treasury would become closer.

In Kissinger's memoirs, he characterizes Connally's negotiating posture: "Connally saw no reason to treat foreigners with any tenderness. He believed that in the final analysis countries yield only to pressure; he had no faith in consultations except from a position of superior strength. His presence as secretary of Treasury guaranteed that the economic dialogue with Europe would not be dull; it also ensured that the European contribution would have to be something more solid than ritual incantations of goodwill."

In the second week of August 1971, Connally informed Nixon that the British ambassador to Washington had paid a visit to the Treasury Department to ask that 3 billion U.S. dollars held by the British be converted into gold. "Connally deferred giving his answer," Nixon says in his memoirs, "but we knew we would very soon have to confront a major crisis concerning the international economic position of the United States."

According to Hendrik Houthakker, a Harvard economist who served on Nixon's Council of Economic Advisers, the British move came in the form of an inquiry "about the possibility of gold cover for their dollar holdings." In Houthakker's view, Connally and other Treasury officials reacted to the move as though it were a direct affront to American dignity and self-esteem. After all, hadn't the United States helped defend the British pound from devaluation in 1964 by purchasing massive amounts of sterling? Although those Treasury purchases had proved fruitless (the pound was devalued in 1967), still, the effort had been made. And now the British wanted the keys to Fort Knox. Was this any way to show gratitude? Connally was incensed. According to Houthakker, the Treasury secretary regarded the British request "as a sign that the international monetary situation was rapidly falling apart."

Nixon got the message. The fate of the dollar was in jeopardy. If the British got their way, their demands would result in a 25 percent depletion of America's gold reserves.

In mid-August, the president called fifteen economic experts, plus White House staff members and a speechwriter, to an urgent secret meeting at Camp David. To conceal their movements and shake off the press, each took a circuitous route to the presidential retreat. They feared that news of an "economic summit" would set off a wave of speculation that could conceivably shut down the entire international banking system. When the group assembled at Camp David on Friday, August 13, both Connally and Nixon made an urgent case for going off the gold standard before the British action touched off a run on gold.

On the evening of August 15, while most of the world's markets were closed, Nixon addressed the nation to report the meeting's results. He announced a ninety-day wage-price freeze, a cut in federal spending and foreign economic aid, and some tax incentives to provide income tax relief, stimulate business, and increase spending on domestic products. But the most sweeping change had to do with the monetary crisis.

Nixon blamed "speculators" for "waging an all-out war on the American dollar." He announced that the dollar would no longer be convertible "into gold or other reserve assets except in amounts and conditions determined to be in the interest of monetary stability and in the best interests of the United States. . . . Now this action will not win us any friends among the international money traders," Nixon continued, "but our primary concern is with the American workers, and with fair competition around the world."

Nixon's announcement delivered the jolt that the

president and his Treasury secretary most keenly desired. The so-called "gold window" was now officially closed. The dollar was free to "float"—which meant it was also free to sink, unless the major nations took measures to support it. The Bank of Japan took in nearly $4 billion as it tried to hold the yen to its parity to the dollar. In the end, the Japanese had to give up and let the yen float, but central bank interventions continued. (The Japanese press began calling the U.S. Treasury secretary "Typhoon Connally.")

This concerted, and ultimately futile, effort to buy up dollars was essentially a duplication of the action undertaken earlier by the Bundesbank. Again the dollar was for sale: there was oversupply as investors began buying up other currencies that seemed likely to appreciate against the greenback. The Bank of Japan was using the only countermeasure available—intervening to sell yen and foreign-currency reserves for dollars in an effort to prop up the currency with artificial demand.

It didn't work. "By the end of August," noted Robert Solomon, the Federal Reserve Board's top international economist, "all major currencies except the French franc were floating, but exchange controls were in widespread use and central bank intervention was substantial." The next four months Solomon would later call a "period of turmoil, both in financial markets and in the political and economic relations among countries."

The unilateral U.S. action—bypassing, as it did, the Bretton Woods agreements—told other nations that they could either repeg their currencies or else live with the reality of a floating dollar. As might have been expected, the foreign powers agreed to negotiate. They were urged into unanimous action by Pierre-Paul Schweitzer, managing director of the IMF. On August 19, he sent messages to all members urging "prompt, collective, and collaborative action to reach agreement on exchange rates." Schweitzer warned that unless prompt collective action were taken, "the prospect before us is one of disorder and discrimination in currency and trade relationships."

As a prelude to his next step, Nixon asked Secretary of State Kissinger to meet with French President Georges Pompidou on neutral ground, the Portuguese island of the Azores. The French were notorious "goldbugs." Gold had sustained the French currency throughout times of war, peace, and neighborly European friction. When the French could cash in their dollars for bullion, they had done so. If the world's currencies were going to be cut loose from gold, Pompidou had to feel that his francs were resting on something almost as solid. If the French objected to the new system, in all likelihood so would representatives from other countries. Conversely, if the French went along, so would the others.

Normally, discussions about monetary matters

would have been conducted between French Finance Minister Valéry Giscard d'Estaing and U.S. Treasury Secretary John Connally. But Pompidou and d'Estaing were political rivals, their relationship was strained, and Pompidou insisted on carrying out these key negotiations himself. On the U.S. side, even Nixon recognized that Connally was not the diplomat of the hour. The role of negotiator fell to Kissinger, who in Nixon's view was a suitable surrogate for Connally.

Kissinger considered himself a "neophyte" in monetary matters. "Even in my most megalomaniac moments," Kissinger later reflected, "I did not believe that I would be remembered for my contributions to the reform of the international monetary system."

Meeting for breakfast on the sunny verandah of the French president's villa in the Azores, Kissinger and Pompidou spent a pleasant morning discussing their currencies. The big question in Pompidou's mind was what the new exchange rate for the French franc would be. That afternoon, Pompidou and Kissinger conferred with Connally and Nixon; then Kissinger privately briefed the president and the secretary of the Treasury. The following morning, Kissinger flew by helicopter to the villa for another breakfast. He and Pompidou dickered a little more about francs versus dollars, then shook hands. A total readjustment of the world's monetary system was a done deal.

Of course, there was the slight formality of getting all the other nations to agree. The key players were the world's ten leading industrialized nations, plus the Swiss, the world's bankers. At Nixon's behest, the so-called Group of Ten met at the Smithsonian Institution in Washington, D.C., on December 16, 1971.

Connally got his chance to wave the big stick. The goal of the meeting, Connally reminded the representatives, was to agree on new exchange rates. The dollar was about to be unhooked from gold. That was a foregone conclusion. If they didn't reach agreement, the U.S. currency would go into "generalized float." Their alternatives were either quick agreement or extended chaos. Bullied by the United States and knowing that the French had already agreed in principle, the other representatives performed as programmed. Soon the finance ministers were quibbling over mere percentage points. Where would the yen be set? What was to be the price of pounds versus deutsche marks versus Swiss francs versus dollars? It was foreign-exchange trading in microcosm, on a diplomatic level, with each minister vying for a little advantage in the world market.

The biggest change was in the drastic upward revaluation of the yen—16.9 percent—which would make Japanese exports far costlier than they had been previously. In 1971 Japan was a rising sun again, with rays of technological power touching all points of the globe.

But the yen was still pegged to the funny-money era of cheap Japanese exports, when it had taken a pile of yen notes to equal a dollar. A 16.9 percent adjustment for the Japanese was drastic. It meant they were out of the fledgling stage of their economic development and coming into the big time. It was the price of progress.

So the once level playing field had turned into a treacherous mine field. The dollar would indeed "float." For the moment, other currencies were "pegged" to the dollar at levels that were presumably fairer than the levels of three days before. The Group of Ten agreed that their central banks would make a sincere attempt to hold their currencies within 2.25 percent of the agreed-upon parities.

What they all conveniently ignored was that the parities were unenforceable. Even in 1971, all the combined reserves of all the central banks could not control currency flows, given the volume that was being exchanged among countries. There was now the potential for massive flight from a currency—with the implied possibility of a currency-market collapse.

Nixon, however, believed the crisis had been met. Standing beneath the Wright Brothers' plane at the Smithsonian, he announced "the most significant monetary agreement in the history of the world." What was most significant about it—though Nixon failed to take note—was that the agreements were meaningless. Once the dollar went into what John Kenneth Galbraith called "atmospheric ventilation," the whole system was likely to come unhinged.

When inflation roars ahead in Brazil, the world's monetary system suffers hardly a blip's worth of change. When Argentina's inflation hits the triple-digit range, the impact on international currencies is negligible. But when the U.S. inflation rate doubles in one year—as it did between 1972 and 1973—and the dollar is floating, the impact on the world's currency markets is enormous.

By the middle of 1973, the terms of the Smithsonian Agreement were obsolete. The agreement was never formally terminated. It just ceased to be relevant in the real world. Washington had abandoned its struggle to stabilize the ever-weakening greenback. All the major currencies (sterling, French and Swiss francs, deutsche mark, Canadian dollar, and yen) were actively traded by international bankers, brokers, and treasurers. At the Smithsonian meeting in 1971, the Group of Ten had set a goal of keeping currencies within a range of 2.25 percent of their pegged exchange rates. By the end of 1973, that goal was a joke.

Governments in Europe and Japan tried to support the dollar, but all the combined powers of the world's central banks could not keep the dollar near the artificially high levels agreed upon at the Smithsonian. Domestic inflation, combined with increasing deficits, steadily eroded the dollar's value. The German mark, pegged at 3.66 to the dollar in 1971 when the float began, would never see that level again. By 1974 it had soared to 2.4 per dollar, an appreciation of 34 percent. When the yen stood at 360 to the dollar in mid-1971, the Japanese government had maintained that its currency would not be revalued under any circumstances. By early 1974 the yen went to 280, a change of 22 percent. (By 1979 the figure would be 180—exactly double its 1971 value.) In December 1971 the Swiss franc was worth 3.94 to the dollar. Three years later, the dollar had dropped to 2.55 Swiss francs, and by 1978 it was nearly 1.62—less than half its 1971 valuation.

In late 1973 the price of crude oil quadrupled. A torrent of cash from the world's industrialized nations flowed into the OPEC countries. For a while, OPEC wealth was exploding at the rate of $50 billion per year. Nearly all those petrodollars came from the Group of Ten nations. The need to stabilize currencies was now overwhelmed by the urgent necessity to pay for oil to keep the industrialized nations running. As Robert L. Bartley, editorial page editor of *The Wall Street Journal*, pointed out in a 1990 commentary in that paper, the "oil crisis" was actually a foreign-exchange crisis. Five weeks after Nixon closed the gold window, representatives of the OPEC nations, meeting in Beirut, resolved that any devaluation of the dollar would be offset by hiking the dollar price of oil. Middle East leaders agreed that they would adopt "ways and means to offset any adverse effects on the per barrel real income of Member Countries resulting from the international monetary developments as of 15th August, 1971." In other words, if gold went from $35 to $350 an ounce, a barrel of oil would simply cost ten times as much. The OPEC message: if the dollar were going to inflate, the price of oil would not be far behind.

The language of the OPEC agreement could not have been plainer. As Bartley pointed out, when the dollar went *off* the gold standard, oil went *onto* the gold standard. Relative to the value of gold—which the OPEC countries held as their standard throughout all the currency fluctuations—the price of oil rose only briefly, then fell to its previous level, and finally (by 1988) fell to bargain-basement prices.

Prior to 1969, when gold was still worth $35 an ounce, a barrel of oil cost $2.75—so an ounce of gold bought 12.73 barrels of oil. By 1969 an ounce of gold bought 13 barrels of oil, and by 1972 an ounce of gold bought 16 barrels. Then the price did indeed go up: By 1976 an ounce of gold bought only 8.84 barrels. But within the next ten years, oil prices fell to 33 barrels per ounce of gold. (Incidentally, the sharp rally in oil prices following the August 1990 Iraqi invasion of Kuwait simply brought the gold-oil relationship roughly back into line with the pre-1969 levels.) The "oil sheikhs" weren't gouging the industrial nations when they raised the dollar price of oil; they were simply responding to the plummeting dollar by putting oil on a "gold standard."

During those anxious days of the oil crisis, estimates of anticipated economic damage fluctuated wildly. Robert S. McNamara, president of the World Bank, was perhaps the chief alarmist. He predicted in 1973 that OPEC's income would be $300 billion by 1980. (In real terms, it ended up being about half that.) As the OPEC countries used their petrodollars to buy property and invest in banks, Western nations feared that it wouldn't be long before oil-producing nations "owned the world."

Italy's economy, already shaky before the oil crisis began, hovered on the verge of bankruptcy. In Great Britain, the value of sterling took a nosedive as OPEC nations yanked their funds out of England and shifted to dollar accounts in New York and to Swiss franc accounts in Zurich. Japan was still economically strong, but it too was at the mercy of OPEC prices. An ever-rising percentage of its GNP was pouring into the Middle East to import oil reserves that would keep the Japanese economic juggernaut running.

By 1974, most countries wanted their currencies to be undervalued, as this would enable them to lower the prices of goods they offered for sale to the United States. That way, they could continue to expand their export base and further stimulate their domestic economies. Naturally, the income of surplus dollars they earned helped pay for their rising fuel costs.

In the United States, inflation reached 12 percent in 1974. But foreign nations that exported goods to America and imported oil for domestic manufacturing tried to support the dollar. They purchased dollars through the central banks to pay for oil, using their own currencies to make the purchases. By generating an oversupply of their own currencies while increasing demand for the dollar, they created a net effect of global dollar support.

9

Brave New World

With the establishment of the Smithsonian Agreement of 1971, the burden of currency risk abruptly shifted from governments to businesses. New institutions had to be created in response to the sweeping changes in currencies and currency markets. As U.S. banks and multinational corporations expanded overseas and the European and Japanese currencies began to float, currency trading became an everyday function of doing business. In international transactions, those who didn't protect themselves from currency fluctuations were cutting their own throats. In a world where the price of sterling, marks, or dollars might change drastically in the time it took to write a contract or pay a bill, the *timing* of any currency transaction had a disproportionate impact on profitability.

Consider the position of an American multinational firm that wanted to build a new plant in France in the 1970s. If Generola Corporation had the on-hand capital (in U.S. dollars) to build that plant, a key question was when to pay for it, and in what currency. Assuming Generola was a large-scale multinational corporation with its own currency department, the corporate treasurer had to consider a number of currency-exchange alternatives before he settled up with his French contractor.

Suppose the total cost of the plant that Generola wanted to buy in France was figured at 120 million French francs. Now suppose that on the day the agreement was signed with the French contractor (who naturally wants to be paid in francs), the exchange rate was 6 francs to the dollar. If this were a world of stable currencies, the Generola treasurer could have written checks totaling $20 million anytime during the life of the contract and still end up paying exactly 120 million francs to the French contractor.

But after the Smithsonian Agreement, such monetary stability was gone. In the real world of currency dealings, the exchange rate of U.S. dollars for French francs could have fluctuated drastically during the time it took to build the plant. If the franc rate had changed to 8 to the dollar during plant construction, then the dollar cost would have ended up being $15 million rather than $20 million. The corporate treasurer was then in a pile of trouble if he had bought all his French francs at the beginning of the project: by doing so, he burned up $5 million of Generola capital to no advantage.

But what if the franc went the other way—perhaps 4 to the dollar by the time the plant was finished? In that case, the treasurer should have bought all his francs at the beginning of the project, when he could have purchased them for a mere $20 million. (If he waited until the end, those same 120 million francs would have cost the company $30 million.) If he gambled right and bought in advance, he would succeed in saving the company $10 million. Promotion time!

It was a lady-or-tiger dilemma. Hedging future prices of currency—such as the "buying forward" policy described in Chapter 3—became a business necessity. It may seem that corporate treasurers were responsible for being prescient, but their number-one requirement was to make sure there were no unpleasant surprises. Opportunity costs were generally much more palatable to senior management than surprise losses and project overruns.

The difference between the "old days" and the "new days" of doing international business was that the corporation and its treasury now had greater risk to manage. Generola could no longer rely on any government or governmental body to defend currency rates throughout the life of a project. In this sense, the Smithsonian Agreement was perfectly fair: It pulled the rug out from under everyone. The 1970s was the decade when, in the international arena, currency speculation became virtually indistinguishable from sound monetary practice.

In this new atmosphere, forward trading flourished, as might be expected. Thousands of Generolas all had the same dilemma—how to stay profitable in their international markets while currency risks were continually shifting. Floating exchange rates also prompted a predictable increase in spot currency trading. Alert dealers in the financial capitals of the world found that they could earn profits for customers, investors, banks, and themselves by buying low and selling high during the trading day. Of course, they could also lose money on the spot market. But the advantages were too attractive to resist, and customers demanded foreign-exchange services. Every bank that wanted to compete internationally was forced to establish an active foreign-exchange trading room just to remain competitive with other banks. When a client called for a price on marks, sterling, or yen, the bank that wanted to provide full service had to be ready to deal.

After 1971 U.S. banks became increasingly involved in the international fray of foreign trading. Previously the center of currency trading had been London. Gradually that honor became shared with New York. To avoid

U.S. controls, many banks set up offshore units where currency deposits would earn higher interest rates. In New York, banks began hiring British traders to teach the Americans; soon the currency-exchange market was thriving on Wall Street as well as in London, Paris, Zurich, and other foreign banking centers. Later, Tokyo, Singapore, and Hong Kong started expanding; soon they were thriving currency trading centers.

The volume of trading altered the relative power of the central banks, because their foreign-currency reserves did not expand at the same rate as the market. Professor Ian Giddy of Columbia University has estimated that between 1970 and 1973, the volume in foreign-exchange trading soared from $25 billion to more than $100 billion in daily transactions. In this larger market, central bank intervention did have an impact, but it was less predictable than before. If the Bundesbank bought hundreds of millions of dollars in exchange for deutsche marks, it might help support the dollar, but on the other hand, the dollar might continue to fall. Further, if the dollar did continue its descent, the only alternative for the Bundesbank was to (a) continue its intervention program, risking still more of the German nation's reserves; (b) sit on its hands and watch; or (c) shut down the market.

In June 1972 the British pound came under pressure when Denis Healey, the shadow foreign secretary, made the rash statement that sterling would soon have to be devalued. During the following six days, there was massive selling, the pound spiraled downward, and the Bank of England spent about $2.6 billion in the market trying to defend the British currency. Rather than exhaust Britain's currency reserves any further, British authorities finally let the pound float.

In early 1973, when there was massive speculation against the dollar, Japan tried to support the greenback against the yen by purchasing $1.1 billion in a nine-day period, but its efforts were unsuccessful. To forestall chaos, the Tokyo market closed. Europe soon shut down as well. Paul Volcker, then chairman of the New York Federal Reserve, made a whirlwind 31,000-mile trip to Japan and the financial capitals of Europe. When he returned, he announced a 10 percent across-the-board devaluation of the dollar. (So much for the 2.25 percent solemnly agreed to at the Smithsonian!)

On March 1, 1973, after the U.S. merchandise trade figures were released, the European central banks bought nearly $4 billion to try to shore up the weakening currency. For the second time that year, the markets closed down. They were to stay closed for more than two weeks while a series of consultations about international monetary reform took place among the Group of Ten nations.

The question facing the industrialized nations was: How could the theoretical parities established in the

Smithsonian Agreement be maintained in the face of uncontrolled speculation? Central bank intervention could go only so far. If central banks had to shut down the market every time currencies went outside their parity ranges, the market would be closed more often than it was open. And this would defeat the very purpose and ultimate good of the market, which was to provide ample liquidity for commercial transactions among nations.

During the two and a half weeks the market was closed, discussions among economic ministers pointed to the conclusion that floating exchange rates were a necessary solution to currency-market woes. Clearly, currency values could not be "pegged," because there was no viable means of enforcing pegged rates. On a floating system, the market—not governments—would determine currency-exchange rates on an hour-by-hour, day-by-day basis.

When the market reopened, "the float" was officially accepted, even though many economic ministers considered it a temporary solution. But the temporary solution turned into the $700-billion-a-day foreign-exchange market that is in existence today.

Between 1974 and 1977, the U.S. economy went into a deep slump. Unemployment remained high, and the American consumer was getting squeezed—so there was less to spend on imports. But even though the domestic economy was shrinking, the United States was increasing its volume of manufactured goods for export. In 1975 there was a small trade surplus of $9 billion. The relative lull and the brief period of dollar stability that prevailed in 1975 and 1976 came to an abrupt end in 1977 with a speech by W. Michael Blumenthal, President Carter's new secretary of the Treasury. On June 24, 1977, at the headquarters of the Organization for Economic Cooperation and Development (OECD) in Paris, Blumenthal suggested that Germany and Japan should increase their imports of U.S. products. He further recommended that the dollar be allowed to decline until prices of U.S. goods were competitive with prices of foreign competitors' goods.

Blumenthal's objective was clear: let the yen rise until a Japanese car cost as much as an American car; let the mark rise until German steel cost as much as U.S. steel. Although Blumenthal's challenge was couched in the language of economic diplomacy, his message was blunt: "Exchange rate adjustments should play their appropriate role." Word that Blumenthal was "talking down the dollar" spread rapidly from the OECD to bankers and traders around the world. Now a U.S. Treasury secretary was *creating* a new source of currency risk.

At first there was some skepticism that Blumenthal meant what he said. But further statements from the

Treasury Department gave credence to the view that Blumenthal wanted the dollar devalued. The immediate reaction to his announcement was an absolutely massive wave of dollar dumping.

Since most countries had currency reserves in dollars, when the dollar lost value, they became poorer. This global deflationary process also applied to the OPEC countries, whose newfound assets (upward of $100 billion) were invested in dollar-denominated holdings throughout the world.

Traders were having a marvelous time, but until the dollar found some support, every country with U.S. dollar reserves would end up with diminishing assets. As the United States continued its currency "management" program, European and Japanese governments intervened, buying the dollar to try to prevent its value from plunging further. By the end of 1978 the foreign-exchange market was again nearing the panic stage. In the single month of October 1978, the dollar sank 6 percent against the Swiss franc, 7 percent against the yen, and 12 percent against the mark.

When 1978 came to a close, the world's standard currency was worth, across the board, about 60 percent less than it had been fourteen months previously. Any Swiss banker, German industrialist, or Japanese manufacturer foolish enough to have held on to American dollars following Blumenthal's talk in Paris was now, respectively, in global terms 73 percent, 62 percent, and 47 percent poorer.

Finally, on Wednesday, November 1, 1978, President Carter announced a "dollar defense package." Under G. William Miller, the newly appointed chairman of the Federal Reserve, the Fed would use a "war chest" of foreign currencies worth $30 billion to mop up some of the billions of dollars sloshing around in the market. On November 1, the Fed spent $300 million per hour while intervening on the currency markets. Traders were initially skeptical, as they had been bearish on the dollar for so long that it was difficult for them to alter their bias. Yet within two weeks the dollar rallied from 1.70 to 2.00 marks as many holders of short-dollar positions were forced to buy them back. The traders had turned into Fed watchers.

The Fed kept up the pressure. An additional $7 billion worth of foreign currencies was spent in November and December. But intervention began losing its impact. American inflation was still rising in double digits, and investors continued to dump dollars. Gold became the great refuge. As the dollar remained weak, gold prices soared to unprecedented heights.

While it had been easy enough to "talk down" the dollar, restoring confidence in the greenback was another matter. Trust in U.S. monetary policy had been seriously eroded during this chaotic period. Beginning with the announcement of the Smithsonian Agreement in 1971, the United States had led the march into world-wide inflation and uncertainty. International economic cooperation hit a new low as Washington demonstrated that, given the right circumstances, it would allow the dollar to plummet with sickening speed. Without any meaningful international cooperation, there was unfettered expansion in speculation, offshore banking, and the Eurodollar market.

Indeed, when it came to shoring up the dollar, the United States had left most of the responsibility to foreign governments. It was only to avert worldwide panic that Washington finally intervened. International monetary policy had fallen backward from the idealistic days when economic representatives had gathered at Bretton Woods. Three decades later, there was nothing left of the currency-exchange sections of the agreement that Keynes, White, and the others had struck. The world's currencies were under the control of a new system in a brave new world that might best be described as random monetary crisis management.

10

The Floating Dollar

TODAY, THE WORLD has readjusted to a new system of foreign exchange. Though the floating exchange rates were initially regarded as temporary, by the early 1980s it was clear that this "nonsystem" was likely to be self-perpetuating. Unless the world's leaders could reach another Bretton Woods–style agreement, the era of pegged rates was over.

In April 1981, four months after taking office, President Ronald Reagan announced that the United States would not intervene in foreign-exchange markets "except in extraordinary cases." During the next six months, while the dollar steadily appreciated, no currencies were bought or sold by the Federal Reserve Bank of New York, the usual conduit for foreign-exchange trading activities. While the dollar continued to appreciate steadily against other leading currencies during the next four years, the United States staunchly held to Reagan's noninterventionist policy. Between 1981 and 1985 the Treasury intervened only ten times, and the net intervention was less than $1 billion.

In retrospect, there are a number of reasons why the dollar strengthened during this era. Under the Reagan administration's loose fiscal and tight monetary policies, spending increased sharply while inflation rates declined. Between 1981, when Reagan took office, and 1984, when he was reelected, the U.S. federal budget deficit soared from $78.9 billion to $212.3 billion. Meanwhile, inflation fell dramatically, from an annual rate of 12.4 percent in 1980 to just under 4 percent in 1982.

Tight monetary policy in the United States meant high interest rates, which lured foreign capital. For a time, the return on investments in dollar-denominated money instruments was far higher in America than anywhere else in the world. During 1981 the Federal Reserve's discount rate reached an all-time high of 14 percent. Federal funds, during the same period, hovered near 18 percent. In 1982, at their peak, long-term rates on ten-year Treasury bonds were over 14 percent. The combination of these attractions, accompanied by government promises to avoid intervention except in dire emergencies, resulted in an unprecedented demand for dollar assets. As the dollar strengthened, investors reaped the double rewards of high yields along with profits in currency transactions.

For five years the dollar was a hot investment item. In 1984, when I began trading currencies on the foreign-exchange desk at Salomon Brothers, traders were convinced you couldn't go wrong buying dollars. While every trader knew this trend couldn't continue forever, the lemming instinct took hold. There had to be a cliff somewhere—but meanwhile, we just kept on running.

Inevitably, the rising dollar had a vast impact on import-export ratios and ultimately the balance-of-trade figures. As the dollar appreciated, imports to the United States became cheaper, U.S. exports more costly in other countries. As a result, imports vastly increased while U.S. manufacturers had an ever more difficult time pricing their goods competitively to sell abroad. As the appreciation of the dollar approached 40 percent, profit margins on export items dwindled away; when U.S. exporters were forced to raise prices, demand for their goods decreased sharply.

The damage showed up in trade imbalances. Using 1982 dollars as a yardstick, the balance-of-trade deficit on merchandise items rose from $28.2 billion in 1981 to $110.2 billion in 1984, an increase of nearly 400 percent. Representatives of corporations and trade groups in the United States began to plead for intervention to bring the dollar down.

One of the prime movers in this campaign was Lee Morgan, chairman of Caterpillar Tractor and chairman of the Business Roundtable Task Force, who launched a campaign in 1981 to realign the dollar against the yen. In 1981 Caterpillar had revenues of $3.5 billion from exports; by 1983 export earnings for the company were just $1.6 billion, less than half that. In those two years the company trimmed 15,000 employees from its work force. "Exchange rate relationships are wreaking havoc on our international competitiveness," Morgan noted in 1984. Morgan and other business leaders, including Chrysler's Lee Iacocca, took their campaign to leaders in the Cabinet and Congress—particularly their plea for a higher yen. Despite their entreaties, and in the face of an ever-increasing trade deficit, Treasury Secretary Donald T. Regan maintained a hands-off policy toward the dollar. By early 1985, at the dollar's peak, its value was 67 percent above the lows of 1980.

Based on the International Monetary Fund's Multilateral Exchange Rate Model, the following graph shows the dollar-exchange rate indexed against other leading currencies for the years 1980–1989:

The dollar peaked and then began its slide in February 1985. That turn, however, was not touched off by any particular event. Throughout the preceding months, leaders of U.S. industry had become increasingly vocal in their concern about the dollar. Unofficially, some

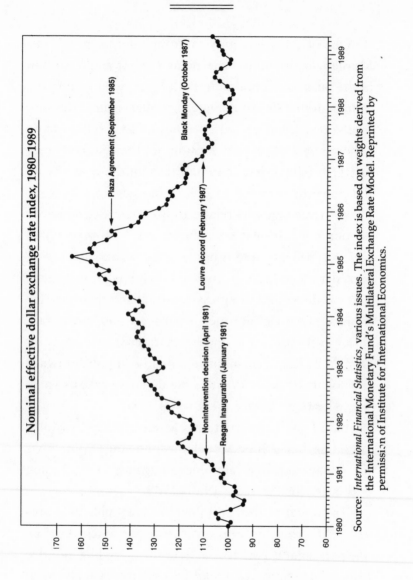

Nominal effective dollar exchange rate index, 1980–1989

Plaza Agreement (September 1985)

Black Monday (October 1987)

Louvre Accord (February 1987)

Nonintervention decision (April 1981)

Reagan Inauguration (January 1981)

Source: *International Financial Statistics*, various issues. The index is based on weights derived from the International Monetary Fund's Multilateral Exchange Rate Model. Reprinted by permission of Institute for International Economics.

Treasury officials seemed to be in agreement. But still there had been no clear signs that the U.S. government intended to intervene in any way to push the dollar lower. As for traders, many thought the dollar was already too high. A downturn was certain, but of course no one could predict when it would occur. Even in retrospect, there is no explanation for the timing of the market reversal.

It was on September 22, 1985, seven months after the dollar began its tumble, that Treasury Secretary Donald Regan met with the G-5 ministers and central bankers at New York's Plaza Hotel. In the announcement of what came to be known as the Plaza Agreement, the G-5 asked for "further orderly appreciation of the main non-dollar currencies against the dollar." Using the word "orderly" in such an announcement was like asking rabbits to ignore a forest fire. The dollar plunged overnight and then kept going. By early 1987 it was exactly where it had started six years previously, when the Reagan administration had announced its nonintervention policy.

In February 1987 the G-5 finance ministers, plus Canada, met at the Louvre in Paris and agreed that the dollar had gone far enough. Although Italy declined to join the Louvre meeting, it later abided by the accord. Thus, all the countries—now seven of them—agreed to intervene. The Louvre Accord resulted in more or less concerted intervention on the part of all the central banks, either through direct dollar purchases or through interest-rate policies. The United States, for example, spent $9.9 billion during the following eleven months in addition to maintaining an unrealistically high interest-rate profile. Once again, attempts at intervention proved futile as the dollar ultimately tumbled through the Louvre Accord levels.

In fact, it was only a relatively short time later that G-7 officials themselves began selling dollars at levels lower than where they had been buying them in their dollar-support program. The central banks' activities were baffling to traders. Presumably, there were policy decisions within the G-7 that could explain such actions. But the net effect was to make traders in the market highly skeptical of policies decided on in G-7 meetings.

The way the authorities used the Plaza Agreement and intervened to devalue the dollar in 1985 was dangerous. Once a trend starts, it often develops a momentum of its own, attracting fresh buying or selling along the way. The market was already taking the dollar down; it was entirely unnecessary for finance ministers to accelerate its devaluation. In a market that's already on its way down, such announcements can create the rush of "a large crowd through a small exit" that, in a worst-case scenario, is impossible to control. All one ends up with is a panic-stricken jumble of crushed bodies.

In 1985 there was a real possibility of free-fall. Traders were so bearish and negative on the dollar that it was difficult even to shift their sentiment to a neutral stance. At the very least, drastic devaluation put us in a position where foreigners had the opportunity to buy American assets at a tremendous discount. With that devaluation we transferred our buying power to the Japanese and the Europeans. When we look at the whole economic scene, the dollar should be worth more than its pure economic value in the United States. The dollar offers enormous market liquidity, political stability, military might and security, tremendous physical and human assets, and financial freedom. It *should* have a premium. The big issue as a trader is how to measure what the economic value is and then determine how large a premium is warranted.

The current nonsystematic approach to exchange-rate negotiation might be called "management by meeting." The basic idea is this: Given the fact that central banks have limited resources, why not have the leaders of certain key nations sit down and talk about exchange-rate policy until everyone can agree to certain terms? Then these individuals should coordinate monetary and fiscal policies in such a way that currencies arrive at certain predetermined levels.

In principle, this would offer a harmonious way to influence a fundamentally chaotic open-market situation. And, in fact, when the leaders, central-bank governors, finance ministers, and adjunct economists of the world's leading industrialized nations gather for brunch, lunch, dinner, (sometimes) golf, and (always) lengthy discussions, they usually come to the hors-d'oeuvres tray or table with the best intentions of improving economic relationships.

At the G-10 meetings, now held annually, the turnout is tremendous and the talk covers everything from the health of the European Economic Community to the new muscle of the South Korean won. It is the smaller groups, however, that tend to focus on specific foreign-exchange issues and problems.

The core group is the G-5—the United States, France, Great Britain, Japan, and West Germany, holders of most of the industrialized world's aces. They have the biggest banks, the largest GNPs, and generally the hardest currencies. The G-5 began meeting in 1975. There are no records of many of their early discussions. In recent years, however, each reunion has been closely monitored, both inside and outside. G-5 meetings sometimes end with minor announcements that have little impact on market behavior. Or, depending on the conditions and status of the markets, announcements by the G-5 may send shockwaves throughout the financial world.

In 1985 Italy and Canada began campaigning in earnest for seats alongside the exclusive five. Their efforts paid off, and the G-7 was created in addition to the G-5, so that there would be meetings enough for everyone. When the G-7 was created, some further goals were specified, most pointedly "a request to the seven finance ministers to review their individual economic objectives and forecasts collectively at least once a year, using the indicators . . . with a particular view to examining their mutual compatibility."

In addition to the G-10, G-7, and G-5, there is also a G-4 (known in the slang of the financial press as the "Gang of Four") comprising bank officials, governors, and representatives of the Bank for International Settlements from the United States, Japan, West Germany, and Switzerland. The G-3 is West Germany, the United States, and Japan; the G-2 is made up of just the United States and Japan.

While all these group meetings have the flavor of excess, they are collectively the only intergovernmental body that can potentially exert much influence over currency-exchange policy. The United Nations, of course, does not have any mechanism for handling such grand economic issues as exchange-rate structures; the World

Bank and the International Monetary Fund have not been up to the task. So it has been left to ad hoc meetings of the leaders of the industrialized nations to attempt to influence the market.

In the United States, explicit authorization for foreign-exchange intervention is technically in the hands of the Treasury. The Gold Reserve Act of 1934 created an Exchange Stabilization Fund (ESF) expressly to enable the Treasury to intervene in the market when necessary to stabilize the dollar. According to that act, the ESF is under the exclusive control of the secretary of the Treasury, "subject to the approval of the President."

The Federal Reserve Bank of the United States is not licensed to set foreign-exchange policy. When the Treasury intervenes, however, it has to use the facility of the Fed. In particular, the purchase and sale of foreign currencies on the open market is implemented by the Federal Reserve Bank of New York. While the Fed doesn't have explicit authority to play this game, ever since the early 1960s, when the Fed stepped in to defend the dollar and the U.S. gold reserves, the Treasury and the attorney general have issued a number of legal decisions that have given the Fed the right to proceed.

It's a strange system. Theoretically, the Treasury and the Fed *could* go their separate ways if they so desired. The Treasury could buy dollars through the Exchange Stabilization Fund while the Fed was selling dollars through the Federal Reserve Bank of New York. The Treasury secretary has to report only to the president. The chairman of the Federal Reserve, once appointed by the president and confirmed by the Senate, doesn't have to report to anyone except his own board, the Federal Open Market Committee, and ultimately Congress.

In practice, the Treasury secretary and the Fed chairman generally behave with reasonable, if not excessive, respect for each other. Traditionally they lunch together about once a week. Both are sensitive to the fact that open disagreement would spread chaos through the system. So the Fed chairman usually pays a visit to the White House before fiddling with interest rates or monetary policy, and the Treasury secretary generally does not make (openly) derogatory remarks about the actions of the Federal Reserve.

This is not to say that the Treasury secretary does not sometimes exert powerful political pressure on the Fed chairman regarding monetary policy. Depending on political pressures, strains on the economy, and the health of the dollar, Fed-Treasury relations can definitely become strained. There are times when Fed policies push the dollar one way while Treasury policies seem to be nudging it the other, spreading bewilderment among investors. At other times, the Fed and Treasury work together—in a manner of speaking—in ways that may risk billions of taxpayers' dollars.

11

The Force

ALTHOUGH THE foreign-exchange market has periods of aberrant behavior, over the long term it can be a strict and ultimately unforgiving disciplinarian. The decline of the dollar from 1985 through 1990 was a reminder to the United States—if any reminder was needed—that it was about to be disciplined for its chaotic, contradictory, and ultimately destructive economic behavior during the 1980s.

Such disciplining would have been unthinkable in the post–Bretton Woods and pre-Smithsonian world, when the dollar ruled international commerce. But dollar dominion no longer exists. Today, the world's leaders in investment, finance, and industry have their choice of strong currencies. While the dollar still has an edge, it is likely to become progressively less powerful in the coming decade as capital investment moves out of the United States and into other strong-currency nations.

Investors recognized that during the 1980s excessive government spending in the United States had been largely supported by foreign capital. Europe and Japan had invested their massive capital surpluses in U.S. Treasury notes and securities. Direct investment in U.S. corporations also increased. By 1986 foreign-controlled firms—led by companies from Britain, France, West Germany, and Japan—held 9 percent of all U.S. corporate assets. Four percent of American workers were employed by foreign-held companies, which accounted for 10 percent of all sales in the United States. When the dollar entered a period of relative stability after the 1987 stock-market crash, interest rates were high, which attracted further dollar-denominated investments and deposits. By 1988 foreign direct investments in the United States were flowing in at the rate of $41 billion a year.

Throughout the 1980s, West Germany and Japan had built discrete empires of capital reserves and had solidified their trading relationships to the point where the dollar was an article of convenience rather than necessity. Germany, at the hub of the revival in Western Europe, had an economy that was largely independent from U.S. trade. Japan in the late 1980s definitely needed the United States as a market (40 percent of Japanese exports went to America), but it was shifting toward sufficiently large domestic demand and consumption and held enough large reserves of yen and other currencies to absorb the shock of an export-market decline and weather a short-term depreciation of U.S. assets.

By 1990 the United States was no longer the engine that powered the international economy. The government had blundered by not accumulating surpluses during the country's growth cycle, because fiscal expansion would then have been a viable way to "spend" the country out of its recession. Given the strength of the German and Japanese economies, investors had every reason to flee the dollar and find refuge in deutsche-mark-denominated and yen-denominated markets. Even those optimists who trusted in the long-term recovery of the U.S. economy were strongly tempted to move their capital into deutsche mark, yen, or other hard-currency strongholds while the United States put its house in order. It seemed prudent to diversify one's reserve currency holdings, particularly as Germany and Japan became magnets for capital that would be used for regional expansion and growth.

A number of factors, however, prevent flight from the dollar. For one thing, close to 70 percent of the world's trade is still denominated in dollars. Dollar-denominated assets are held not just by U.S. citizens but by investors of every nationality. When the dollar weakens, the stated value of these assets is correspondingly reduced. To the extent that the world's markets continued to be dominated by goods, investments, and services that are measured in dollars, the term of measurement—that is, the dollar itself—continues to retain its value. Rampant devaluation would hurt all the owners of dollar-based assets—and so the market has a built-in incentive for halting a drastic decline.

In addition, there are weaknesses inherent in the economies of both Germany and Japan. For instance, consider the reservations of an investor looking at the West German economy at the end of 1990: By the end of the decade, West Germany had shared its deutsche mark with East Germany, whose economy was in worse shape than that of many Third World countries. Between August 1989 and August 1990, East German industrial output decreased 50 percent—and the West German Finance Ministry was estimating that output would fall an additional 15 percent by August 1991. East German unemployment stood at 130,000 in June 1990, shortly before unification; by November that figure was 1.5 million. Potential downward pressure on the mark was exacerbated by increasing economic, political, and social turmoil in the Soviet Union.

As long as Germany struggles with the costs of unification, it continues to risk inflation—an especially serious concern for the Germans, considering their wrenching experience with hyperinflation following the

First World War. In many respects, Germany holds the key to opening Eastern Europe. But before the benefits of new trade opportunities can be realized, the infrastructures of the former Iron Curtain countries need to be rebuilt in a new form. Given the uncertainties of the rebuilding process—and those nations' unfamiliarity with the fundamentals of capitalism—Germany faces political and economic struggles that will affect the value of its currency at least through the next decade.

There are also some questions about Germany's much-vaunted ability to maintain its lead in industry. As Japan and the Pacific Rim countries have begun to monopolize the trade in new technology, Germany has failed to keep pace. Traditionally, its strength was in industrial reliability; Germany was a workhorse, not an innovator. In the new global economy, market leaders must be innovative in order to remain competitive. Will Germany keep up?

The uncertainties of absorbing East Germany could create exactly those deficits that Germany most urgently wants to avoid. The fact is that those deficits could total in the trillion-mark range. In 1990 anyone taking a long-term view of the dollar—allowing for the mysterious but oft-proved ability of America to recover from precarious positions—would have ample reason to have a constructive view of the mark for the next four years, and then look for a corrective, adjustment phase to the capital inflows generated by loose fiscal policy and tight monetary policy.

A 1990 investor comparing the Japanese yen to the dollar and deutsche mark would find ample reasons to be somewhat wary of the Japanese currency as well—but for different reasons. By the end of 1990, Japan visibly had its share of potential and actual economic problems. With nearly 40 percent of Japanese exports directed toward the United States, the yen was safe only as long as the U.S. recession did not exceed certain limits. Should Japan lose a large portion of its U.S. export business, however, drastic readjustments would have to be made in the Japanese economy. Japan urgently needed to initiate a significant amount of trade with Western Europe, which had already proven its willingness to use protectionist measures to exclude the Japanese. Unless Japan could find other buyers for its export items, its marketplace would become seriously constricted by a U.S. recession.

In addition, Japan had a number of other looming problems that could destabilize the yen. From December 1989 to the same month in 1990, Tokyo share prices had fallen 40 percent exposing serious deficiencies in the Japanese financial structure. Much of the Japanese stock-market speculation in the late 1980s had been fueled by the inflated value of Japanese land and property. Many Japanese commercial banks, like their American counterparts, had huge exposures in land and property development schemes. Prior to the spring of 1990—when the Nikkei took its sharpest plunge—banks, financial investment companies, property development companies, and individuals were borrowing heavily against inflated property values in order to play for high stakes on the soaring Japanese stock market. The result was a highly leveraged financial system.

Throughout the 1980s, Japanese banks were significantly undercapitalized. Although by the end of 1989 most of Japan's big banks had achieved the 8 percent capital ratio required by the Bank for International Settlements, the criteria for "capitalization" were dubious. Under Japanese regulations, big banks could count 45 percent of their "hidden assets" as capital—assets that are largely comprised of stock-market holdings. (Most Japanese banks use specially designated funds, the *tokkin*, to camouflage their exposure in the stock market.) As a result, when the Nikkei plunges, the portion of bank "capitalization" based on stock market speculation takes a serious beating. Should this highly leveraged banking structure take further losses in the 1990s, the whole financial system would be under tremendous pressure. If the Japanese were to move into a recession and bankruptcies of financial institutions began to proliferate, systemic weaknesses would quickly come to light.

Concerns about the general health of the Nikkei also restricted the maneuverability of monetary authorities in Japan. During the 1980s, the booming Tokyo stock market became an investment vehicle for everyone from individual housewives (who purchase stocks from door-to-door securities brokers) to pension funds, banks, and such "nonbanks" as leasing companies, credit-card firms, and consumer-finance companies. With that kind of involvement in the stock market, Japanese authorities find it difficult to impose strict money-tightening measures. If the authorities were to raise interest rates too high in an attempt to choke off inflationary pressures and lower overinflated land values and asset prices, then Japanese housewives and institutional investors might be prompted to flee stocks and reinvest in money-market instruments. Should that happen, the Nikkei would plummet even farther than it did in 1990.

Japan's level of government spending was another factor that could potentially undermine the yen. By the end of 1990, the Japanese government was in debt about 165 trillion yen—$1.2 trillion—with a commitment to increase its debt load even further. At the "structural impediments initiative" (SII) talks with U.S. trade officials in June 1990, the Japanese government agreed to significantly upgrade and modernize its infrastructure. By the end of the talks, Japanese officials had agreed to raise the level of public spending from 6.7 percent of GNP to 10 percent of GNP within five years. Under the SII plan endorsed by the United States, the Japanese government committed itself to spending an estimated 500 trillion yen during the coming decade on such projects as roads, sewers, parks, bridges, telephones, railroads, and airports.

To international investors, Japan's inflated property assets, shaky stock market, bank weaknesses, and government indebtedness were all "warning signals" about the Japanese economy. Yet there were compelling reasons why the yen should remain strong. Japanese industry was superbly capitalized, with more than 90 percent of capital spending by Japanese firms being internally financed. Further, despite stock market uncertainties, the nation continued its remarkable growth, with domestic consumption remaining sufficiently high to attract foreign capital. New capital inflows, in turn, fueled Japanese expansion in the three regional growth blocks of North America, Europe, and Asia, further boosting the Japanese capacity for global production and distribution.

Despite ongoing concerns about the deutsche mark and yen, the dollar of the early 1990s obviously has strong competition from other currencies. Today, international investors have at least a three-way choice. As we enter the last decade of the century, it is clear that the dollar's fate is being determined more by the decision making of global investors. Those choosing the most prudent course can now select from three "reserve" currencies, rather than just one.

12

The Boiled-Frog Syndrome

VIEWED FROM ONE perspective, all the worst things that could happen to the dollar have already happened. From another, the worst is yet to come. In the 1960s it was unthinkable that the United States would go off the gold standard. If we did, what then would "back" the dollar? How would the international balance of payments be settled? What would prevent the Treasury from flooding the market with currency—printing more dollars, willy-nilly, any time they were needed?

But we went off the gold standard and the currency survived. Why? In part, because the U.S. dollar was already the international currency—the standard currency used to settle accounts between nations and to pay for the goods exchanged across international borders. Hence, the dollar, which had no value in terms of being backed by gold, retained much of its value simply as a standard of international settlements. At this point, the premium value was built into the dollar. Dollars were highly regarded in countries with weaker currencies— and therefore the premium was paid. Ironically, the dollar held its premium value in nations that had stronger or equally strong currencies, simply because they needed its international buying power. It was not as good as gold any more, but it served an essential function. The world was politically and economically dominated by America, and the dollar reflected that hegemony by serving as the primary instrument of international transactions. People were willing to pay a premium just to have its liquidity.

The United States, in turn, honored its role as the holder of the international currency. It had few limitations on trade. Anyone with dollars could come to the great American market and purchase goods for their home economies. (We welcomed the export business.) But the free-trade policy went far beyond the buying and selling of goods. Foreign investors and speculators could also buy pieces of U.S. public-owned companies. They could buy Treasury notes. They could invest in real estate, build factories, and sell goods within U.S. borders to U.S. citizens, while taking the profits back home.

This free-trade policy was generous in one respect, but in another it was simply pragmatic. Trade was as beneficial for the United States as it was for the nations that traded with this country. The American consumer welcomed many foreign products, from Dutch chocolates to Japanese VCRs. The benefits spread from the purchaser—who got a quality product at a lower price—to the importer who handled the product and ultimately to the American worker, who began to get jobs in foreign-owned businesses on U.S. shores.

Foreign investment in U.S. financial markets was also an open-door activity. Although some corporations grew uncomfortable as greater proportions of their stock went into the hands of foreign buyers, the foreign activity ultimately benefited share prices—so the gates were left open. As for the foreign purchase of U.S. Treasury notes, it turned out to be an excellent way to finance government spending, whether for defense, social services, or savings-and-loan bailouts.

All these activities supported the dollar. Although the transaction might begin and end in a foreign country, any dealing with America meant dealing with the dollar—and that meant dollars had to be bought before goods, property, or financial instruments could be purchased. It was the gateway, the means of access, to America's riches; and everyone who passed through the gateway had to pay the price for the ticket. So the price of the ticket remained high. As long as it remained the standard international currency, the dollar did not need gold backing any more than an American Express Gold Card needs gold behind it. Purchasing power was everything.

In this way the dollar survived the first of the "unthinkables." Going off the gold standard, it ran into some bumps and hurdles. But it did not undergo a calamitous collapse. Internationally, governments, citizens, and institutions still wanted it; and as long as there was demand, it held its value.

Then came the eighties, and the second "unthinkable" occurred. The United States became a debtor nation. Now, surely, there would be flight from the dollar. Didn't the adverse balance-of-payments situation and the soaring government debt mean that the United States would ultimately be unable to pay its bills? Would its creditors not be left holding worthless sheets of paper promising payment they would never receive?

Strictly speaking, yes, this was the meaning of international indebtedness. Had there been another currency with the same liquidity and buying power ready to take the place of the dollar in the 1980s, perhaps there would have been a flight from the U.S. currency as soon as it became apparent that the United States could not meet its obligations. But no alternative existed. Central banks around the world held large amounts of their reserves in dollars. Multinational corporations did much of their banking in dollar denominations. Abiding by the strict definition of indebtedness, the United States could not pay its bills; on the other hand, it was unthinkable that all creditors, domestic and foreign, would rise up at once to demand payment. Further, so many worldwide investors and institutions held the U.S. currency that a precipitous run on the bank would have been counterproductive and self-destructive (assuming it could somehow be engineered).

So the second unthinkable came and went, and those who warned of a currency Armageddon were either disappointed or simply amazed that the whole structure did not fall apart.

Having survived that, what could be the next disaster—the one that would *really* bring the U.S. Treasury to its knees?

Clearly, that crisis would be a steady and prolonged devaluation of the currency. If the dollar were to decline to a sufficiently low level against the other leading currencies of the world, surely investors would begin to flee to sounder currencies outside America. As the dollar plummeted, the flight would turn into a rout, the rout into a panic. In the worst of all possible scenarios, inflation would soar as the dollar sank: American citizens would enter the twilight of impoverishment as foreign exporters of technology, services, and resources (the pedestals of world trade) began to refuse dollars and ask for deutsche marks and yen instead.

But that particular doomsday scenario didn't become a reality either. When, between 1985 and 1987, the dollar fell close to 30 percent against the world's other leading currencies, business continued almost as usual. True, foreign companies had trouble keeping their price tags competitive in the United States. On the other hand, they saw more opportunities to buy "bargain" goods (including land, banks, factories, farmland, film companies, and assorted corporations) at lower dollar prices than ever before. The dollar was honored throughout it all. Not for an instant did Saudi Arabian princes, Baltic industrialists, Singapore manufacturers, or London security brokers think of refusing dollars. Dollars were certainly worth less; but they were always accepted (and almost invariably preferred) nonetheless.

So the third "unthinkable" event had occurred— and no disaster resulted. Anyone working on a dollar-doomsday scenario was hard-pressed to figure "What next?" With the ever-increasing balance-of-trade deficits, the mounting government debt, and a huge devaluation, the troubled greenback looked as if it had been through everything—and survived, intact, as the accepted international currency of settlement.

Meanwhile, as the S&L crisis, the Gulf War, and the largest government deficit in the history of mankind all gathered on the doorstep of America, the $700-billion-a-day foreign exchange continued to wax hot and cold over the dollar in fairly normal ways. True, the entire foreign-exchange market could collapse. Any unregulated market can do that. But free-fall conditions had come and gone before. Why shouldn't the dollar survive it all?

It is said that there are two ways you can try to boil a frog. One way is likely to be unsuccessful: If you boil a pot of water and drop in a live frog, the frog will immediately leap out of the pot. No boiled frog.

The other technique is to put the frog in a pot of room-temperature water and place the water on the stove, gradually raising the temperature. Being cold-blooded, the frog will become accustomed to the increasing temperature of the water. By the time the water reaches boiling temperature, the frog's body temperature will be the same temperature as the water. Lulled into complacency, it expires.

This is "the boiled-frog syndrome."

Had we gone off the gold standard, plunged into debt, and devalued the dollar by 50 percent in the span of a few months, we would unquestionably have realized we were in boiling water. But these events occurred incrementally. At each stage, the United States (and other nations dependent on the dollar) had a reasonable period of time to adjust. Nonetheless, there are many signs that we are in boiling-water conditions.

The Boiled-Frog Syndrome

Not only the value but the status of the dollar has changed drastically in the past twenty years. At first the change of status was almost imperceptible. Now it is becoming increasingly clear that the new status of the dollar will have a profound effect as the United States conducts its political and economic affairs during the next score of years. In the new world where investors have an increasing number of choices, they may still select the dollar as the currency of convenience, but it is likely that they will further diversify their use of the dollar as the currency of investment. And there is an increasing danger that those who hold on to the dollar without recognition of the risks may end up like boiled frogs.

13

One Nation, Under Debt

WE ARE GENERALLY unfamiliar with the sight of the United States as a debtor nation, but the current decade is likely to acquaint us with all the ramifications of that newly acquired status. The overall deficit incurred in the 1980s will certainly have a permanent effect on the status and behavior of the dollar.

To appreciate the effect of debtor status, we need to see America from the point of view of an international investor. Assume for the moment that you are an investor in early 1991 and you have three choices—a $1 million purchase of assets in the United States; a DM 1.65 million purchase (worth about $1 million in 1991 U.S. dollars) in West Germany; and a ¥ 138 million purchase of financial assets (about $1 million U.S. dollars) in Japan. Assume further that the costs of borrowing money for each purchase are roughly comparable. Which would you prefer to own?

In the past, international investors clearly leaned toward the dollar-denominated property. That is, given a "basket of currencies" to invest in, nearly 70 percent of assets would be placed in dollar-denominated deposits. Why?

To use a real-estate analogy, the neighborhood was good. Geographically, the United States was isolated from the Cold War center of East/West Europe; from the instabilities in Southeast Asia; and from the territorial feuds of the Middle East. The United States represented a nation of continuous growth and reinvestment, political stability, vast natural resources, military strength, and huge market liquidity. International investors holding surplus dollars were readily available, so dollar-denominated assets could easily be transacted at some fair price.

These factors helped give the dollar its premium value. It was reasonable to assume that the million-dollar property could be resold at a profit that would more than cover the cost of dollars used for investment. From an international perspective, investors counted on continued inflation of prices in the United States as well as the liquidity of U.S. assets. When the United States was a creditor nation, such investment was not exactly risk-free, but the appearance of risk was certainly minimized.

Just as a house buyer in the suburbs could look back at five decades of unbroken increases in property values, so the international investor could look at an equivalent period of steadily increasing U.S. asset values.

Likewise, because the dollar had its premium value, investors tended to tolerate a degree of low productivity that would have been unacceptable in a less well established economy. For instance, given an equal opportunity to invest in a plant in Brazil and a similar plant in the United States, the international investor would be far more likely to select the U.S. plant even if it were less productive. The inherent low-risk advantages of the American system dominated some of the potential rewards of higher returns.

In this benign climate, even nonperforming assets in the United States had a higher international value than highly productive assets in many other parts of the world, based simply upon location. Again, the simplistic analogy of real estate applies here: As long as there are people willing to buy at a higher price, the perceived value is more important than the actual "performance" value. As any realtor will testify, the three things that matter most are location, location, and location.

Problems with location began to arise in 1990 as the American economy entered a recession. A new question faced investors: What happens when dollar-denominated assets begin to *depreciate* in value?

The first change one notices is a subtle shift in the proportions of assets held by international money managers—whether individuals, banks, corporations, or investment firms. Although the shift in asset holdings may be incremental, such changes can have a disproportionately large effect on relative currency values, especially when the impact is multiplied by the actions of many thousands of such investors worldwide. The perceived "flight from the dollar" could be precipitous. If millions of investors around the world were motivated to relinquish their U.S. assets, the move would have a profound impact on *the perception of the value* of U.S. assets. Prices that are already headed down will continue to fall faster and farther. Once prices begin to fall, there is no motivation to reinvest. A condition of an ongoing, "rolling" depreciation is created.

During the 1980s, the United States depended on foreign investment to finance the nation's growing debt burden. This the international community was willing to do—particularly from 1985 onward—partially because of the steady inflation of asset values, partially because of attractive interest rates, and partially (at times) because of a favorable exchange rate. But what happens when the United States enters a period of deflation? As international investors unload dollar-denominated assets and increase their investments in Germany, Japan, and other hard-currency nations, what is likely to be the long-term effect on the U.S. economy?

In the world of flourishing international opportunity, where investors have many choices among many currencies, the flow of capital will invariably go into those economies whose asset values appear most likely to increase. It is probable that, over the long run, creditor nations like Germany and Japan will continue to attract investors while the giant debtor nation, the United States, is likely to see confidence eroding as investors shift from assets that are steadily declining in market price.

In such a climate, an added disincentive to international investors is the continued decline of the dollar. When the extent of the dollar decline matches the return from interest rates, the net return on investment reaches zero.

This international situation does have some precedents. Certainly there have been times when investments in other nations' assets looked more attractive than investments in the United States. What is unprecedented is the total debt burden of the United States, combined with its reliance on foreign investment, its direct competition with two other strong economies, and the general uncertainty about the soundness of U.S. government policies.

To complete the picture, we must ask how the U.S.-based investor will react to the devaluation of domestic assets when he has the choice of trading dollars for other

hard currencies and investing overseas. At home in the
United States, an investor caught in a recession is confronting deflation on many fronts. His real income is
declining and his primary assets are declining in market
value, yet he must continue to pay principal and interest
on notes that are denominated in prior years' dollars.
Turning to the yen or deutsche mark, he begins looking
for overseas investment opportunities: To the degree
that he reduces his dollar portfolio and increases his yen-
or deutsche mark–denominated assets, he is "selling"
dollars. When thousands of investors are selling dollars,
the result is a further decline of the dollar in speculative
markets and a further depreciation of U.S. assets. The
international worth and buying power of the United
States and of all holders of dollar-denominated assets is
reduced.

Thus, while capital flight might be initiated by foreign investors, the continued flight is likely to be rein-
forced by their counterparts in the United States. In a
deflationary market, paying off old debt in predeflation
dollars becomes exorbitantly expensive. Better to drop
those assets as soon as possible and find other opportunities elsewhere in the world.

Indirectly, the United States would benefit from si-
multaneous recessions in Germany and Japan. Then, at
least, investors would be motivated to hedge their investments in yen- and mark-denominated assets by retaining

a foothold in the U.S. economy as well. But despite the structural problems in the economies of these countries, it seems unlikely that recession will grip them in the same way it has the United States.

Before the advent of the Gulf War, there was the hope in some circles that the United States would put its financial house in order by reducing defense spending, increasing incentives to invest in productive capital assets, reorganizing the banking system, expanding co-operation with trade centers in Europe and the Pacific, and enhancing its educational system. The war, how-ever, set the U.S. economy on a regressive course. It dramatically made evident the deep-seated weaknesses in America's financial condition as the United States was forced to beg from its allies the wherewithal to finance its military operations. Sadly, the United States appeared to the rest of the world as a skillful mercenary. Whether America can successfully shift to a savings-and-invest-ment economy from a consumption-based one is un-clear.

By the early 1990s it was apparent that Japan would insulate itself from the U.S. depression by expanding into other markets, reducing its reliance on U.S. trade, and decreasing its holding of U.S. money instruments. These tactics, combined with Japan's refusal to make a major commitment of funds to the Gulf War, served to insulate the Japanese economy from many of the U.S. economic woes, at least for the time being.

Germany left itself open to the possibility of rampant inflation in its support of the East. By 1991, however, European economic unification—an event that would provide a considerable boost to the overall German economy—was only a year away. With unfettered access to markets throughout Western Europe, the German industrial state could count on continually rising demand until at least the middle of the decade. Far less dependent on the U.S. market than in previous decades, Germany might face a recession of its own; but in all likelihood it would be unrelated to the U.S. economy.

It is possible that the international investment community, through foreign exchange, may succeed in imposing a discipline on U.S. government spending and asset management that we have failed to impose on ourselves. Ongoing deflation (the cause and perpetuator of any depression) will lead to ever-increasing defaults on debt, as the United States begins to pay for the speculative frenzy of the 1980s characterized by takeovers, excessive consumer spending, reckless investments by the banking community, and the escalation of commercial-property speculation.

The currencies of nations in which these excesses did not occur will become increasingly attractive to a more discriminating international investment community. If the perception ever arises that the U.S. government has fully abandoned its responsibility to the domestic economy, the traditional confidence in the dollar will become a thing of the past. The international investor will have little incentive to pay a premium for a currency that once represented security, liquidity, and stable government, if in fact all three of these "premium values" are put into question.

In the 1990s trading among currency holders is more likely to be driven by a pragmatic assessment of the foreign-exchange market and rival economies than by the historical role—and therefore the psychological primacy—of the dollar. It is unlikely that money dealers on the streets of New York will ever swap soft-currency dollars for hard-currency yen or marks in back-alley trades. On the other hand, the economic equivalent may begin to occur in the capacious boardrooms of the largest multinational corporations as corporate treasurers state that they are beginning to prefer the deutsche mark or yen as a form of payment—just to be on the safe side.

When that begins to happen, the final curtain will be drawn on Bretton Woods. What was once the world's currency of choice will have become merely another currency of convenience. When the world's international investors find that it is no longer convenient to trade primarily in dollars, a great deal more than preferential status will be lost. We will be forced to face the reality of our status in the world, question our economic values, and ask ourselves how we can best market our assets to an international community of discriminating buyers.

14

Living with Uncertainty

WE HAVE LEARNED to live with uncertainty. Everyone who has international dealings—from the transcontinental frequent flyer to the treasurers of multinational corporations—has learned to live with an ever-fluctuating currency. To a degree, we have an adequate flexible-response system to a highly variable exchange-rate system. We even attempt to profit from the speculative opportunities that are now built into the system.

But the world as a whole is suffering from the inefficiencies of an improvised system. Investors have learned to cope by implementing stopgap measures; but what we need for long-term economic planning is an international currency that has a value that is in some way linked to the economic realities of trading nations. We are hedging and hoping, but we aren't answering the fundamental question: How do we build a sounder system of currency exchange?

One of the peculiarities of today's chameleon dollar is that it not only changes value from hour to hour and day to day, it also has an ever-changing value in terms of usefulness. If you are traveling in the Soviet Union with dollars, for instance, you will quickly discover that the U.S. currency has a utility value far above the stated exchange rate. It opens doors, eases transactions, and generally makes life more pleasant for the American traveler (or any other traveler in the Soviet Union who happens to be carrying dollars). In other words, the dollar displays a utility value far in excess of its official exchange rate.

Ever since the dollar became *the* international currency, there has been an inconsistent relationship between its utilitarian value and its value as the world's most widely traded commodity. In its most simplistic form, the utilitarian value adds up to what economists express in terms of purchasing power parity—PPP. Theoretically, they ask, what does it cost to purchase a "basket of goods" (consisting of mixed technological products, foodstuffs, and amenities) in Germany, Japan, England, the United States, etc.—expressed in the respective currencies of those countries? If you can calculate *that*, economists figure, you know what the true value of each currency should be. Having done these

calculations, economists and Treasury ministers are be-
mused by the fact that the traded values of currencies
deviate widely (and usually arbitrarily) from the closely
calculated PPP values. (*The Economist,* wryly, has devised the Big Mac measure of the PPP: What does it cost
to purchase a Big Mac in each currency? Since a Big Mac
is the same the world around, *The Economist* argues that
this standard commodity is a perfectly suitable currency
parity index. And, in a blow to higher econometrics, it
turns out that *The Economist* Big Mac index is usually
within a few points of the parities established by the
more elaborate PPP.)

While it is natural to yearn for a simpler econometric
model in which currency values are mathematically ad-
justed according to the PPP index, the reality is that the
"basket of goods" is not much more than an illusion. A
basket that contains a Sony TV, a Honda Accord, and
a bowl of rice is not the same as one that holds a GE
television set, a GM car, and a Coke. Technology makes
a difference. So does culture. So does the consumer's
perception of the basket of goods. In the import-export
business as well as in the world of international capital
investment, all these factors alter the perceived value of
the basket—and commensurately, the utility value of the
currency that buys the goods in that basket.

If the world wants American products, goods, investments, and services, the utility value of the dollar is likely

to remain high. Dollars need to be bought in order to buy goods in the basket; hence a high demand for dollars. But if the U.S. basket becomes less than desirable for some reason (and desirability is largely—but not completely—a function of perception), there is likely to be a commensurate loss in the utility value of the dollar. Less demand for the product means less demand for the currency that purchases the product.

But ever since the float began, the dollar has acquired a speculative value that is partially or totally dissociated from its utilitarian value. For instance, in a climate where balance-of-trade figures consistently show consumers preferring European and Asian goods over U.S. goods (because of price, perceived quality, or any other reason), the value of the dollar as a speculative instrument can fall ever lower.

If the U.S. Treasury's view of the dollar appears at times to be arbitrary and contradictory, the reason may be that there are, at any given time, almost equivalent reasons for wanting the dollar to rise and wanting it to fall. In early 1991, for instance, central bank intervention was a bit confused, with the authorities first selling dollars, then buying dollars, then selling them again. It seemed as if they were not quite sure what they wanted.

Traders, as usual, did pay attention to Fed intervention (or its absence); they listened to Federal Reserve Chairman Alan Greenspan's announcements (and noted his moments of silence); they watched U.S. interest rates fall and the economic situation deteriorate. But their behavior had little to do with the economy. When the Gulf War ended and the stock market surged, they rushed out and bought dollars as though they were the rarest of baseball cards.

The laissez-faire policy toward the dollar—and the free-market-style foreign exchange—are entirely consistent with the venerated principles of American free enterprise. The question is whether these principles will work effectively (not to mention efficiently) in a world where international controls are needed to prevent a crash of the foreign-exchange market.

The foreign-exchange market is often regarded as though it were an institution devised by sage finance ministers and heads of state for the benefit of international trade. In fact, it is no such thing. It is an improvisation at best. As the world has shrunk, communication has accelerated, settlements have become more rapidly paced, and the foreign-exchange market has certainly become more technically proficient. But for all its apparent efficiencies and the gravitational mass of its $700-billion-a-day volume, it is still a loose cannon.

Interestingly enough, this is precisely the kind of improvisation that disappeared from the United States with the creation of the Federal Reserve System in 1913. With the issue of Federal Reserve notes, a currency was created that would have the same value in any state in the union. Trade within the United States was no longer a swap-meet among holders of different currencies; instead, a single dollar could be exchanged for goods, products, and services. The states were finally united economically as well as politically.

Given a world united by trade and diplomacy, it would seem sensible to end the money bazaar by creating an internationally recognized currency. Yet, assuming we continue on the current track, that seems hardly conceivable. Just as the U.S. Constitution predated a U.S. currency, so too an internationally recognized currency would have to be preceded by the creation of a globally recognized central bank governed by an internationally appointed board of directors.

The great economies of the world are unlikely to be that closely united. Instead, we see increasing movement toward a tripartite world with currency loyalties divided among Europe, Japan, and the United States. By January 1, 1994, the European Community plans to have a European central bank as the first step toward a single currency, the European Currency Unit (the ECU), although Germany will likely dominate the economic scene. Meanwhile, the Pacific Rim will be dominated by the yen. That leaves the dollar to play a role in the Americas. (And probably a large proportion of Third World nations will be dominated by U.S. dollar transactions.)

How will this increasingly tripartite structure change the stature and power of the dollar? Will the United States find itself in the position of having to pay off its debts?

One of the givens of a multinational power is that it cannot default on its debt. There are an almost infinite number of refinancing schemes available when one controls the currency with which the debt is repaid *and* the money supply from which repayments are made. (By contrast, when a Third World nation cannot repay its debt to the United States, its alternatives are limited. Since the debt is invariably denominated in dollars, a Third World nation gains nothing by printing an infinite amount of its own currency; it only creates hyperinflation. Without this alternative, its only recourses are to vastly increase its exports, to take out further loans from other nations—which are understandably reluctant to lend to a country that has defaulted on earlier debts— or to reschedule its debt-repayment plan.)

For the United States to go into default is "unthinkable"—yet, like other unthinkable currency events of the past two decades, it could happen. Nonetheless, it would take a curious form, since in this case the debtor nation controls the money supply that repays the debt. Theoretically, the United States could just print whatever money is necessary to settle the account. Foreign investors who purchased government notes would earn precisely what they were promised—the only problem being that the dollars in which they would be repaid would be worth vastly less.

If this decision ever were to be taken, there is little that could be done to stop the ensuing inflationary spiral. If an overabundance of dollars floods the market at the same time the dollar is falling, it will become apparent to investors that there are better things to do with their capital than to refinance the U.S. debt. Lack of foreign investment will impose fiscal austerity on the United States on a scale that this country has been able to avoid up to now.

The increasing incentive is for foreign capital actually to take over U.S. production facilities—from farms and factories to financial services and stockyards. This certainly occurred in the 1980s. But it is unlikely to happen again—at least on an equivalent scale—if the dollar steadily declines. If dollar profits cannot be taken out of the United States at a favorable rate, foreign investors will find it difficult to justify new purchases of U.S.-based assets.

Can the United States become accustomed to being a partner among equals in the global economy—or are we locked into a leadership role, even if the role is meaningless and the leadership is lacking? There is no agenda for the dollar. And even if there were, we would not have any means of implementing or enforcing that agenda. Not only that, there are no meaningful plans to enact new policies—or, for that matter, to develop fiscal and monetary policies that will benefit the United States and, in the long run, the world. In theory, the initiative for new resolutions on global currency issues could come from the United States. But the United States in its current weakened economic position has no way to launch those initiatives without incurring a political risk.

No matter how willing we are to advise other nations on their trade and domestic policies, we cannot avoid the fact that the United States is in the midst of an economic mess. After a decade of dramatic underinvestment and overconsumption, a tremendous effort will be required to set the United States on a feasible, constructive, long-range program of correcting the excesses of the 1980s. The danger is that in certain ways it is inordinately convenient to have a dollar unhinged from the fundamentals—a dollar that can rise or fall on the foreign-exchange market with only grudging and inconsistent government intervention. In certain ways it makes perfect sense politically that Washington is maintaining a basically hands-off policy toward the dollar—since excessive government manipulation is likely to create negative results at some level of the economy. Conveniently, we can always say that it is historically defensible to leave the dollar at the mercy of free-market forces.

Nonetheless, it would be a delusion to pretend that continual neglect of the dollar will ultimately lead to sounder international relations. True, a rising dollar has lured foreign investment and enhanced the international buying power of the United States, while a falling dollar has boosted our exports. Both views have been explained, justified, and ultimately endorsed by parties defending U.S. interests. But now we need policies that will give the dollar renewed stability as the international currency of choice—to allow economic activity to thrive in an atmosphere of diminished uncertainty. Until now, leadership has not taken the necessary steps to establish those policies. Holding dollars is now more of a gamble than it has been at any time since Bretton Woods.

Conclusion

As we have seen, the foreign-exchange market was the result of convenience rather than design. By 1973, when all the major currencies began to float, global trade was expanding rapidly. The international banks were already servicing increased demands for liquidity, and all the major players in foreign-exchange transactions had lines of credit with one another. European bankers, especially, were adept at borrowing and lending in foreign currencies. In other words, conventions for efficient trading in floating currencies were already established.

But, as we have also seen, the foreign-exchange market was never incorporated or chartered to perform any specific functions. To this day it has no headquarters and no official bureaucracy. The centers of this market remain diversified, and to a large degree its operations are improvisational. Essentially, there are as many foreign-exchange operations as there are computer display terminals and telephone hookups. Each trader defines his or her own rules—though all are linked to the same network and all conform to certain protocols.

Because of its noninstitutional structure, the foreign-exchange market is exposed to certain risks that would probably be lessened were it to operate under the scrutiny of an international watchdog agency of some kind. On the other hand, its very lack of institutional boundaries allows it a flexibility that would be absent were it to follow strict controls and guidelines.

There is at least one clear danger: that a "run on the market," foreign-exchange style, could cause a near-total collapse of international liquidity. The nightmare described at the beginning of this book is certainly possible. Such a drastic event as a devastating Tokyo earthquake *could* lead to repatriation of the yen, which would be disastrous worldwide. A run on any of the major currencies would have severe consequences, but the damage from a collapse of liquidity in the dollar would be the worst.

On the other hand, the foreign-exchange market has shown notable resiliency during a number of tests—including oil shocks, U.S. and Japanese stock-market collapses, the reunification of East and West Germany, the Gulf War, sharp trade imbalances, and numerous economic fluctuations of a lesser nature.

A market collapse, if it were to occur, would probably follow from overspeculation in one currency, leading directly to a condition of gross under- or overvaluation. As we have seen, this is what happened in general to the dollar in the mid-1980s. Like any other commodity that is heavily traded, currency responds to demand, which creates a rise in prices that in turn leads to further buying. Speculation has its own momentum, and habits take over. Just as no one knew where the dollar would peak in 1985, no one can say how high is too high, once the market begins developing a trend in a certain direction.

At some point there will always be a turn in the market. Traders will get caught in unprofitable positions. But whether or not that turn is damaging to global trade and harmful to economies in general depends on how abruptly the price adjustment to the overspeculative condition occurs and the percentage of change from the high to the low. The span of the rise and fall of the dollar in the 1980s took six years. Had the same peak and collapse occurred with greater velocity within a shorter span of years, there is no telling what kind of economic conditions we would be seeing today.

Risk also increases to the extent that money is borrowed on margin. One of the leading reasons given for

the 1929 stock-market crash is that numerous speculators were able to buy securities with very little cash
down. When the market crashed, they were unable to
meet margin calls from their banks. Bank collapses en-
sued as a direct result of the market collapse. It was a
self-perpetuating nightmare.

Today, internationally, banks have huge exposures
in foreign-currency obligations, including extensive
commitments to make future payments. The system
works as long as the vast majority of participants in the
market can count on liquidity. In other words, if a trader
goes short dollars and long yen in the morning, he does
so with the confidence that even if the market should go
against him, he can square up his dollar position and cut
his losses. This confidence in market liquidity is based
upon his own experience and on past market history. In
recent times there have always been buyers at some level,
always sellers at some other level. As long as this is the
pattern, participants trust the market.

Every trader's activities are supported by his confidence that a nearby exit always exists. Panic occurs when
all doors are closed, or when everyone is headed for a
single exit. The nightmare for any trader is a scenario in
which he offers a currency and no bids come back. He
offers the currency again at a lower level—and still there
are no bids. As his "offered" price falls lower, his view
of the world changes. Instead of facing the possibility

that he might lose 1 percent, 2 percent, or even 5 percent of his investment, he now faces the reality that he may lose 10 percent, 20 percent, or conceivably 50 percent. "Panic" becomes the operative word, because that is exactly what each trader begins to feel upon first confronting the possibility of such losses.

The question, then, is what could create such a sudden absence of liquidity, even on a temporary basis. In an active market where there are steady currency flows, buyers are likely to come in at some level. In the cyclical nature of markets, it is natural to find buyers looking for good value at a low price. But what if high demand is followed by a sudden absence of buyers at any level?

One counteroffensive, in the event of the sell-off of a leading currency, would be corrective action by the central bank of the nation whose currency was under attack. This action would have symbolic importance— as it has in the past when any of the G-10 countries intervened to support currencies. If cooperation were customary among all leading nations, it is possible that concerted buying of billions of dollars' worth of any currency could lead to a short-term solution; but if the central banks used up their currency reserves without turning the market, there would be no floor under the collapsing currency.

A balance of commercial and political powers is vital to maintaining liquidity in the market, especially during times of crisis. The world's leading currencies, no longer backed by gold, are backed instead by the stability of their governments and their economic infrastructures. There is no reason to foresee economic collapse in any of the nations in the industrialized world that back the leading currencies. So free-fall in the market is unlikely. Yet the risk is always there.

Ever since John Maynard Keynes' finest hour at Bretton Woods, there have been strong advocates of a single world currency. In fact, at this point it is a concept with so many benefits that it requires little advocacy. What is lacking, however, is any plausible plan for moving from the current free-market condition into a world where everyone would use a single agreed-upon currency for international business.

What would be the advantages of a single world currency? Most obviously, large reservoirs of doubt would be eliminated from international business transactions. No longer would companies have to hedge future transactions and allow for exchange-rate uncertainties in all their projections. On a one-currency system, for example, U.S. ImportCo could purchase Jaguars in Britain at an agreed-upon price and be assured that no additional costs would be incurred as a result of exchange-rate fluctuations. This would allow ImportCo to make longer-term plans for business, based upon projections of its profit margins. If the price in the agreement of sale was 30,000 in WorldMoney for each Jaguar, then the price of WM 30,000 would hold whether settlement was made today, in three months, or in two years. Ultimately, that would be better for exporters and domestic producers as well. Price adjustments would have more to do with efficiencies in costs and production, rather than shifts in relative currency values. A U.S. manufacturer of televisions, for example, would pay costs in WorldMoney and also set his prices in WorldMoney. To the extent that this manufacturer could lower costs, therefore, he could either increase his margin or price the televisions more competitively.

A single-currency system would also change the flows of capital. Today, when a government significantly raises short-term interest rates, there are usually two effects—a tightening of credit in the domestic economy (because loans for investment become more expensive) and an increase in capital flows into the country (to take advantage of the elevated interest rates). Due to the second effect, investors seeking higher interest rates create demand for the sought-after currency.

Under a WorldMoney system, investors would not sell marks to buy dollars (for instance) just because interest rates in the United States rose. If interest rates in the United States soared, Germans and others would be likely to invest more in U.S. assets, yet the value of the WorldMoney used for investment would remain the same worldwide. Essentially, the whole world would be subject to the same overall rates of inflation or deflation.

For investors using WorldMoney, selecting investments in the global currency would be no more complicated than shopping around for attractive interest rates. If Bank High gives a seven percent return on investment while Bank Low, next door, gives a six percent return, customers will naturally flock to Bank High. Soon Bank Low will be forced to raise its rate to seven percent to stay competitive. So, too, Nation Low would have to keep interest rates on a scale with Nation High in order to keep capital in its economy. The net effect, then, would be an equalization of interest rates internationally, as nations were forced to compete for capital that was the same denomination the world over.

For advocates of a single-currency world, interest rates pose the stickiest problem. If a single currency comes into common worldwide use and is internationally recognized as the only means of account settlement, which government or intergovernmental body will set interest rates? How can a nation maintain control over its own economy if interest rates are "fixed" at a certain level by the market, or by a group of international economists who have the discretionary power to set rates?

Since lower rates generally stimulate economic growth, if all nations were to accept a single World-Money, they would have to relinquish some autonomy. Should interest rates in Japan be the same as those in the United States? If Japanese consumers are saving money, implementing fuel-conservation measures, and steadily increasing production—while the United States continues on a course of consumption and spending, with declining investment and scant increases in production— it is difficult to imagine an interest-rate agreement that would be compatible with both societies.

Resistance to the concept of monetary union in the European Economic Community has highlighted this problem of a single-currency system. Though the arguments for a WorldMoney are compelling and the industrialized nations would benefit in many ways, it is likely to be a very long time indeed before leading nations agree to relinquish control over domestic economic policy by accepting the internationalism signified by a single currency. To many, the establishment of a central bank for the world—which would be needed for a world currency—is tantamount to the establishment of a single world government . . . at best a distant gleam in the future.

In many respects, the foreign-exchange market in its present form is a mechanism ideally suited to respond to global change. Guided by its invincible hand, both the industrialized and nonindustrialized nations of the world are forced to consider their internal disciplines while confronting the realities of the global marketplace. The market itself is extraordinarily fair, in the sense that it has no favorites and every nation is subject to the persistent and equal scrutiny of all participants in the market.

The admitted weaknesses of the foreign-exchange market are those of any market—its tendency to respond to rumors as though they were facts and to turn habits into trends. But along with those weaknesses, this market has astounding strengths. Even under circumstances as dramatic as a Tokyo earthquake, there stands at least a better-than-even chance that the market would find unanticipated ways to rebound, with only temporary impairment of currency flows.

Today, the foreign-exchange market adequately adjusts to the most complex global relationships among private interests and state powers. Its proven ability to respond to crisis has shown that this market can be self-corrective. Yet economic leaders still have a tendency to regard this exchange-rate mechanism as entirely temporary. Whether there is another, more systematic and rational approach to currency transactions that can be ratified by all nations remains to be seen. In the meantime, the unregulated market combined with "management by meeting" is the only mechanism to handle transactions in a floating-rate system.

Perhaps the foreign-exchange market's greatest strength is its freedom from institutional restraints. Institutions are, by their nature, self-perpetuating. The foreign-exchange market is not. It arose from a specific need and despite its massive size, when the need no longer exists, the foreign-exchange market will cease to function in its present form.

It is true, of course, that hundreds of thousands of traders and investors have a direct stake in the market, and many banks rely on foreign-exchange profits to improve their bottom line. Nevertheless, their interests are extremely diversified. If the market were to diminish of its own volition—or if profit opportunities were strategically reduced by imposing limitations on trading—banks and traders would simply adapt to the new conditions. Though obviously there are profits to be made in the foreign-exchange market, it cannot be perpetuated solely as a profit-making vehicle. Its primary function, in the larger analysis, is to provide liquidity for international capital and trade flows.

Given the resiliency of the market, it can adapt and correct itself as international mechanisms of cooperation and trade gradually change. Should the European Economic Community succeed in adopting the European Currency Unit, traders will simply begin trading the ECU against the yen, U.S. dollar, and other currencies. Undoubtedly, adjustments would be necessary; the market would take some time to find equilibrium after such a step. But there is no question that the market could adapt to such a change without significant restructuring.

Similarly, the market will surely adapt to changes in U.S. trade relationships with its neighbors to the north and south. As trade increases with Canada and Mexico, both the Canadian dollar and the Mexican peseta are likely to undergo significant changes vis-à-vis the dollar. While it is impossible to predict the impact of these adjustments, there is no doubt that the foreign-exchange market is equipped to deal with them.

If the foreign-exchange market is indeed a temporary system, it is also an ideal one in the respect that it will cease to exist when there is no longer a need for it. Like a gold-rush town built only for the temporary service of gold hunters, the foreign-exchange market sprang up as a convenience. Should dealing in foreign currencies cease to be profitable, foreign-exchange brokers and traders would turn to other markets, investors would look for more attractive opportunities elsewhere, and banks would seek alternate forms of investment. Like a ghost town after the gold runs out, the foreign-exchange bazaar would be an artifact of a bygone era. Until that day, however, the foreign-exchange market will continue to measure the world's currencies against one another on a scale held by blind justice, perpetually tilted by the warring and complementary forces of supply and demand and guided by its invincible hand.

Sometimes I wonder what I'm going to be when I grow up.

Sometimes I think this is the greatest way to make a living, feed and clothe and educate my kids, travel to places I want to be, make some money, and stay involved in the big game of life.

Sometimes I think it's a stupid way to make a living but a great way to meet bright people who are thinking about the world in about seventy different languages on every continent during most of their waking hours.

Sometimes, when I'm really sleep-deprived and really right and the voices on the phone and the numbers on the screen form an interlocking grid of meaning, I think I am as closely tuned as I can ever be to the world's internal workings, at a level that can be sustained for only short durations.

Sometimes I wonder whether it's really myopic to see the world's workings through the eyes of a trader who always has to be responsible for his profits and losses.

Sometimes I think this market is really necessary to the economic health, balance, and dynamism of the world, that it's the greatest working people's tool since the plowshare.

Conclusion

Sometimes I think it's silly and brutal, that nations and economies get hurt while political and economic leaders make stupid decisions and traders dash to catch an upward trend before it peaks.

Sometimes I'm in awe of the power the market has to self-adjust and assert its age-old force.

Sometimes it amazes me how the market can be tweaked into submission.

But it's not really the flickering numbers that hold my attention, nor the voices on the phone, nor the determination of point spreads, nor the excitement of making profits.

What keeps me at the screen is the most challenging match I've ever played. Sometimes I watch myself playing it and wonder why. But that consciousness doesn't affect the outcome of the match. It only affects the way the game is played.

It is now three in the morning, at the opening of the London market. I'm watching little flickering numbers on the screen and reading stale news bulletins regarding U.N. discussions of economic sanctions in the Middle East.

Could it be that I actually enjoy this?

When something like Iraq breaks on the news, am I getting some sneaking gratification out of playing a bit part in adjusting the world around the event? Why is it so important to me to outguess the London bankers as they step out of their cabs this morning? Why do I feel as if I know what's in the mind of a Singapore trader as he pulls down the shades and falls asleep? Do I really believe I can anticipate the behavior of the Arab emirs as they figure out how to maneuver their armies, manipulate their oil prices, and adjust the disposition of their dollar holdings? Can I figure out what George Bush is dreaming about in Kennebunkport? If he, like me, is staring at a flickering screen tonight, what will he say to the press tomorrow? And what impact will that have on the dollar, mark, yen, and French frank?

I go to the kitchen to get a bowl of cereal.

I come back to the screen.

The deutsche mark is down a pfennig against the dollar in the London opening.

Not completely unexpected.

But what's the *real* reason for that move?

What's behind it?

Why is it happening?

I put down my bowl of cereal and punch a telephone number, dialing London.

A British voice comes through the speaker.

"Hello?"

"Hi, this is Andy. What do you think here? What's going on?"

Index

asset holdings, shift in, 193
Axilrod, Stephen H., 80

bancor, 115–16, 120
Bartley, Robert L., 145
bid, 83–84
Blumenthal, W. Michael, 156–57
Bretton Woods, New Hampshire,
    109
Bretton Woods Agreement, 105–16
    end of, 132
    purpose of, 118–19
British pound, 29
    experience with, 61–79
Business Financing Conference, 129
Business Roundtable Task Force,
    163

cable, 29
capital flows, 46–51
    and commercial trading, 48–51
    and hedging, 49–50
    shifting, 46–47
    short-term, 47
    and speculative trading, 47–48
Carter, Jimmy, 158
Caterpillar Tractor, 163
Chamberlain, Austen, 111
commercial and political powers,
    balance of, 214–15
commercial trading, 48–51
commodity options, 35
Connally, John, 134, 135–39, 141,
    142
corrective action, 214
cover, 32

currencies:
    charts, 43–44, 56
    floating, 132–33
    hard, 14–15
    soft, 14–15
    trading history of, 43–44
    see also currency, single world;
        individual names
currency, single world:
    advantages of, 215–17
    and interest rates, 217–18
    and resistance to, 218

debtor nation, United States as,
    190–99
default, 206–207
d'Estaing, Valéry Giscard, 141
Deutsche mark: see German mark
devaluation of U.S. dollar, 186–87
Dow Chemical chairman, 128–29

The Economic Consequences of the
    Peace (Keynes), 111
The Economist, 202
economy:
    analyzing, 88
    and foreign investments, long-
        term effect on, 193–99
ECU: see European Currency Unit
equilibrium point, 59–60
ESF: see Exchange Stabilization
    Fund
Eurodollar market, 124–29
European Currency Unit (ECU),
    205
Exchange Stabilization Fund (ESF),
    170

Index

exports:
  and foreign-exchange rates effects
    on, 11–12
  import business, 19–20

Federal Open Market Committee,
  171
Federal Reserve Bank of New York,
  170
Federal Reserve Bank of the United
  States, 170–71
  and U.S. Treasury relations, 171
Federal Reserve System, 204- 205
fill, 32
float, currency, 132–33
floating exchange system, 155,
  160–71
foreign-exchange market:
  adapting to change, 220–21
  effects on U.S. dollar, 9–12,
    25–26
  and anticipating trends, 52–81
  beginning of, 149–59
  building a sounder system,
    201–209
  and commodities, bonds, and
    securities, 20–21
  and events leading up to,
    106–16, 122, 123–34
  forms of transactions, 17–18
  as a free market, 21–22
  and free-market forces, 12
  influence, 23–24
  and liquidity, 23
  and strengths of, 219–20
  and terms used in, 29–33
  and weaknesses of, 219
  and who can enter, 15–17
  and why created, 22–23
foreign investment in U.S. financial
  markets, 184
free-fall, 44
free-trade policy, 183–84

G-2 (Japan, United States), 169
G-3 (Germany, Japan, United
  States), 169
G-4 (Germany, Japan, Switzerland,
  United States), 169

G-5 (France, Germany, Great
  Britain, Japan, United States),
  42, 168–69
G-7 (Canada, France, Germany,
  Great Britain, Italy, Japan,
  United States), 169
G-10 meetings, 168
Galbraith, John Kenneth, 121, 144
Gang of Four: see G-4
Genghis Khan, 108
German mark, 29–30
  and floating the, 132–34
Germany:
  and economy of in 1980's, 173,
    174, 175
  and unification of, 175–77, 197
Giddy, Ian, 153
Gold Reserve Act of 1934, 170
gold standard, 107–108
  and abolishment of, 123–34
  abolishment's effect on other
    nations, 139–41
  and events leading up to
    abolishment of, 135–39
Goodman, George J. W., 79, 80–81
Greenspan, Alan, 203
Group of Five: see G-5

hard currencies: see currencies
Healey, Denis, 153–54
hedging, 49–50
hot money, 130
Houthakker, Hendrik, 137

Iacocca, Lee, 163
IMF: see International Monetary
  Fund
import-export business, 19–20
Institute for International
  Economics, 79–80
interest rates:
  real, 53
  and a single-currency world,
    217–18
International Bank for
  Reconstruction and
  Development: see World Bank
international bank plan, 114–15
  discipline in, 116
  see also World Bank

Index

international indebtedness, 185–86
International Monetary and
    Financial Conference of the
    United and Associated Nations,
    105
International Monetary Fund (IMF),
    118, 170
    Multilateral Exchange Rate
    Model, 163
international monetary system,
    reform of, 139–44

Japan:
    and economy of in 1980's,
    173–74, 175
    insulating itself from U.S.
    depression, 196–97
    and level of government spending
    in, 179–80
Japanese yen, 29–30
    and problems that could
    destabilize, 177–80
Johnson, Lyndon B., 135

Keynes, John Maynard, 109–16,
    117, 120–21, 215
Kissinger, Henry, 136, 140, 141
kiwi: see New Zealand kiwi

Lawson, Nigel, 62
Lenin, Vladimir Ilich, 111
levels of resistance, 56–57
liquidity, 23
    maintaining, 213–15
long, going, 30–32
Louvre Accord, 165–66

McNamara, Robert S., 147
management by meeting, 167–69
mark: see German mark
market traders: see traders,
    decision-making process of
market trends: see trends,
    anticipating
markets:
    accumulation and distribution
    phases of, 57–59
    interrelationships of, 28–29
    see also foreign-exchange market
Marshall Plan, 121

Miller, G. William, 158
Money World (TV show), 79
Morgan, Lee, 163
Moscow Narodny Bank, 125

New Zealand kiwi, experience with,
    93–104
Nikkei, 178, 179
Nikko Securities, 80
Nixon, Richard M., 120, 136–37,
    138, 140, 141, 142, 143

OECD: see Organization for
    Economic Cooperation and
    Development
offered, 84
oil crisis of 1973, 145–48
OPEC agreement, 146
options, 33–39
    call, 35, 36–37
    commodity, 35
    mispriced, 37–38
    premium, 36
    principles of, 34–35
    and probable price behavior,
    37–39
    put, 35, 36–37
Organization for Economic
    Cooperation and Development
    (OECD), 156

Plaza Agreement, 42, 165
political and commercial powers,
    balance of, 214–15
political structures, analyzing, 88
Polo, Marco, 108
Pompidou, Georges, 140, 141
pound: see British pound
PPP: see purchasing power parity
prices, foreign-exchange rates effects
    on, 10–11
purchasing power parity (PPP),
    201–202

Quantum Fund, 62, 63

Reagan, Ronald, 160
Reagan's noninterventionist policy,
    160–61
Regan, Donald T., 163, 165

risk-management system, 91–92
rolling depreciation, 193
Roosevelt, Franklin D., 107
run on the market, 211

Salomon Brothers, 27, 95
Schweitzer, Pierre-Paul, 140
short, going, 30–32
SII: *see* structural impediments
  initiative plan
Smith, Adam: *see* Goodman,
  George J. W.
Smithsonian Agreement of 1971,
  142–44
soft currencies: *see* currencies
Solly: *see* Salomon Brothers
Solomon, Robert, 139
Soro, George, 62, 63
Soviet Union, 125–26
speculative trading, 47–48
spread, 32
square, 32
structural impediments initiative
  plan (SII), 179–80
Swiss francs, 29–30

Thatcher, Margaret, 61
Those Swiss Money Men (Vicker),
  125
The Times of London, 15
tokkin, 178
Tract on Monetary Reform
  (Keynes), 113
traders, decision-making process of,
  82–93
  and analyzing economy, 88
  and analyzing world events,
  85–87
  and bids, 83–84
  and following risk-management
  system, 91–92
  and other traders' views, 88
  and own point of view, 89–91
  and political structures, 88
trends, anticipating, 52–81
  and currency charts, 56
  and economic factors, 54
  and finding equilibrium point,
  59–60
  and interest rates, 53

and levels of resistance, 56–57
and market behavior, 57–59
and market history, 55–57
tripartite world, 205–206
Tuttle, Jeff, 63–65

United Nations, 169
U.S. dollar:
  and appreciation and depreciation
  of in 1980's, 41–43
  and devaluation of, 186–87
  dominated assets depreciate,
  192–99
  and foreign-exchange rates,
  effects on, 9–12, 25–26
  and foreign investment in U.S.
  financial markets, 184
  and free-trade policy, 183–84
  as international currency, 182–83
  and international indebtedness,
  185–86
  and speculative value of,
  203–204
  and utilitarian value of, 201–
  203
  and weakening of, 122–23
  and why has survived, 182–89
U.S. dollar defense package, 158
U.S. dollar-exchange rate index
  graph, 164
U.S. Treasury, 170–71
  and Federal Reserve Bank
  relation, 171

Vicker, Ray, 125, 127
Vietnam War, 122, 123
volatility, 35–36
Volcker, Paul A., 135–36, 154

The Wall Street Journal, 7, 15, 125,
  145
White, Harry Dexter, 117, 120–21
Williamson, John, 79, 80, 81
World Bank, 118, 169–70
world events, analyzing, 85–87
world lending organization: *see*
  international bank plan; World
  Bank

yen: *see* Japanese yen